THE OUTLYING FELLS
OF LAKELAND

THE
OUTLYING FELLS
OF LAKELAND

CENTENARY EDITION

being a Pictorial Guide
to the lesser fells
around the perimeter of Lakeland
written primarily for
old age pensioners and others
who can no longer climb high fells
but can still, within reason, potter
about on the short and easy slopes
and summits of the foothills.

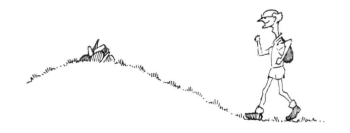

AWainwright

Frances Lincoln Limited
4 Torriano Mews
Torriano Avenue
London NW5 2RZ
www.franceslincoln.com

Originally published by
Westmorland Gazette, Kendal, 1974

First published by Frances Lincoln 2003

Centenary edition with re-originated artwork
published by Frances Lincoln 2007

Printed and bound in Singapore

A CIP catalogue record for this book
is available from the British Library.

ISBN 978 0 7112 2805 4

9 8 7 6 5 4 3 2

CENTENARY EDITION
PUBLISHED BY
FRANCES LINCOLN, LONDON
2007

THE PICTORIAL GUIDES

	First published	Revised
Book One: The Eastern Fells	1955	2005
Book Two: The Far Eastern Fells	1957	2005
Book Three: The Central Fells	1958	2006
Book Four: The Southern Fells	1960	2007
Book Five: The Northern Fells	1962	2007
Book Six: The North Western Fells	1964	
Book Seven: The Western Fells	1966	
Pennine Way Companion	1968	
A Coast to Coast Walk	1973	
The Outlying Fells of Lakeland	1974	

PUBLISHER'S NOTE

This Centenary edition of *The Outlying Fells of Lakeland* is published in the year of the hundredth anniversary of A. Wainwright's birth. It is newly reproduced from the handwritten pages created by the author more than thirty years ago. The descriptions of the walks were correct, to the best of the author's knowledge, at the time they were first published and they are reproduced here without any amendment. However, footpaths, cairns and other waymarks described in this book may change over time and walkers are advised to check with an up-to-date map when planning a walk.

Fellwalking has increased dramatically since the Pictorial Guides were first published. Some popular routes have become eroded, making good footwear and great care all the more necessary for walkers. The vital points about fellwalking, as A. Wainwright himself wrote on many occasions, are to use common sense and to remember to watch where you are putting your feet.

A programme of revision of the Pictorial Guides is well under way, and revised editions of the remaining guides, including *The Outlying Fells of Lakeland*, will be published over the coming years.

THE OUTLYING FELLS
OF LAKELAND

INTRODUCTION

WALK : *The ordinary human gait in which both feet are never off the ground at once.*

WALKING : *The act of going on foot : act of moving with a slow step.*

These are dictionary definitions. They make no reference to the pleasures that can accrue from walking, no mention of the beneficial exercise so gained nor of the satisfaction felt upon reaching a desired objective on foot under your own steam.

Walking comes naturally to all of us. We walk (by roundabout routes) from cradle to grave. For most people walking is, throughout life, a simple means of locomotion from point A to point B, and preferably by the shortest and easiest route. If a car comes along they hop in; might as well save their legs, they say.

A minority, however, walk for pleasure, finding enjoyment as they go along, exploring old haunts and visiting new scenes, developing an awareness of the things around them. Some have a burning curiosity to look round the next corner and some find a supreme joy in attaining remote places.

The best walking is the traversing of terrain that can only be reached on foot, and in country with a crowded network of roads on lower ground this means walking on hills and moorlands that are inaccessible to wheeled traffic and where the only method of progress is by use of the legs — lonely country, inevitably: natural wildernesses where most people wouldn't be seen dead, so they say, and certainly not alive. Walkers who walk for the sake of walking are still, by many people, regarded as crackpots.

This sort of rough tramping has become known, in the last century, as fellwalking. It is not a game, not a sport, not a competing with others, but a pastime: a simple way of spending leisure hours alone or in the company of kindred beings that has as its aim merely the study of nature in some form or other: flora or fauna, geology, the lie of the land; or of sites of antiquarian interest on the hills: old mine-workings, relics of former civilisations, ancient settlements. All harmless pursuits, all instructive. Most fellwalkers become aware of the fascination of these 'sideline' interests but the over-riding impulse generally is to reach a pre-determined objective. The objective is usually a mountain top. Mountain tops are very satisfying. They are well-defined landmarks, usually indicated by a cairn. They are attained only after exercise of the limbs, the satisfaction of surmounting them being in direct proportion to the effort involved — the harder the task the greater the reward, which is as it should be. They are remote, detached from everyday life. They are new viewpoints, reminders of true values, places to refresh the soul, to banish worries, to sweep away the cobwebs that so confuse the urban mind. In a changing world they remain unchanged. In the modern swirl of shifting and transient loyalties they are anchors. One always feels better after climbing a mountain.

Fellwalking is a pastime available to everyone, and unlike games and sports is not restricted to age groups. It is a pastime for the young and the middle-aged and the old; indeed, its attractions actually increase as the years go by. Ardent fellwalkers never give up. They fade away, in due course, surrounded by maps, their gnarled fingers still tracing fresh routes. They die hoping for hills in heaven.

White hair is no deterrent. Retirement from the factory or office is not an end to everything: it is not an end to anything but work. Fellwalking helps better than doctors to keep a man fit, and enthusiastic not only about hills but about life... The satisfaction derived from a successful climb becomes even keener with the passing years.

Fellwalking is a pastime for life.

But — and this is the reason for the appearance of this book — physical and other disabilities may develop in later years. Bodily ailments may occur in spite of healthy exercise: legs tend to become rickety and bones brittle; or a half-century of pipe smoking may play havoc with the wind; or a street accident may curtail freedom to walk and climb in comfort; or over-indulgence in sexual activities may have robbed the limbs of energy (perish the thought, but it had to be mentioned). Or domestic difficulties, an unsympathetic family or a shortage of cash in old age may rule out the longer expeditions. Senile decay may set in but is unlikely in a seasoned fellwalker. Rigor mortis is the one great disability to fear, and avoid as long as possible.

Of this book, as of no other of mine, I can say quite truthfully that it has been requested, and the requests have come from fellwalkers now in the sere and yellow, old-timers who have climbed all the lofty peaks and still cannot be persuaded to send their boots to a rummage sale, whose fires of enthusiasm for the hills are unquenchable, but who for one reason or another can no longer drag themselves up Scafell or Gable yet aren't content merely to sit in the valleys and look up. It suits me to do this book on the lesser fells, since I am in like circumstance, my own capacity for higher climbing being diminished for the second (I hasten to add) of the reasons mentioned above.

HE'LL NEVER DO IT!

.... 200 ....

So I have been wandering of late amongst the foothills of Lakeland, the minor eminences around the perimeter, the little bumps we never bothered about before. Rather unexpectedly, the infants have proved a source of pleasure scarcely less as a class than that afforded by their hoary seniors. A summit cairn at 1000 feet can be just as exciting as one at 3000. As much can be explored in one mile as in five. There are delectable couches on the way up, the sort of natural resting places we used to look at enviously as we toiled past and now at last have time to enjoy. There is a tearoom at the foot of the hill when we feel like going down. There is no hurry. It's great, lounging in the heather just listening to the birds and the tinkle of baby becks, looking across to the mountains of youth from an extremely comfortable and recumbent position. It's great, you tell yourself, to know that there aren't endless miles of mountain and moor and bog still to be crossed before the day is done. Yes, there's something to be said for being old and a little bit doddery. You almost feel sorry for the youngsters sweating up Rossett Gill at this very moment. You tell yourself that these lesser hills are surely to be preferred to the Wasdale giants. You kid yourself..

...... 300 ....

Of the hundred or more fells described in the following pages many are of outstanding beauty. The fascination of limestone is well exemplified on Scout Scar and Whitbarrow. Charm is the keynote of the undulating country around Coniston Water. The Black Combe area provides more serious walks on ground akin to the Howgills, with fine panoramas, and the lonely ridges of Shap Fells will appeal to a lover of solitude. There is no lack of variety.

I have confined the contents of this book to the area within the Lake District National Park (with a few minor variations) otherwise it would be difficult to decide on an arbitrary boundary. Some lesser heights that looked to be worth an exploratory visit have been omitted for reasons concerned with land use: new afforestation (an insidious and growing threat to the freedom of the hills) and cultivation and farming, or with trespass on strictly private ground (which must always be respected). In fact, access to many of the maritime foothills is less easy than it is to the mountains. Some included are difficult to travel upon: being low and sheltered and near the sea they are lush jungles of thick heather and bracken where, if pathless, progress is not only slow but fraught with minor perils. But most are simple walks without hazards. Some involve fairly long expeditions and may prove formidable for pensioners not in peak condition. Most, however, are short, and start and finish at the same point to suit those (now a majority) who take to their feet from a parked car.

The problem of arranging the chapters in some semblance of order, a logical sequence, has been overcome, somewhat erratically, by starting in the southeast, at the foot of Long Sleddale, and proceeding clockwise around the district. The foothills are abundant in the east, where they merge in the Pennines, and in the south, where they decline to the sea, but they are few and far between in the west and north, where the high fells descend abruptly to the coastal plain. This gives the book a decided bias in favour of east and south. But that's the way the land lies.

In a sense, this book is a mopping-up operation. It draws into the net those modest eminences that escaped inclusion in the seven pictorial guides to the higher fells of Lakeland. There are enough of them to provide an extended lease of activity for semi-retired fellwalkers for a few more years. I hope it does this. And helps to make the last years the best.

But remember...... you are not as young as you used to be.

You might come across me on Orrest Head someday, gazing over the lake to the Langdales. Or, more likely, halfway up, resting and having a pipe....and wishing I was fifty years less old.

aw

November 1973

THE CHAPTERS IN THE BOOK
in the order in which they appear

Diagram showing the distribution of the outlying fells included in this book in relation to the Lake District National Park boundary (x×x×x×x)

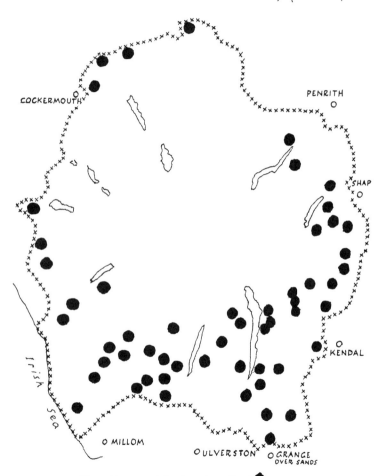

PENRITH

COCKERMOUTH

SHAP

KENDAL

Irish Sea

O MILLOM

OULVERSTON

O GRANGE OVER SANDS

The odd man out is Humphrey Head

Details of the fells commence overleaf. Each is the subject of a separate chapter (including also any subsidiary fells) with a description and map of suggested walks.

The fells are arranged in a geographical sequence, i.e. clockwise from the southeast. This arrangement makes quick reference less easy than an alphabetical sequence would but has been considered the best to adopt because many of the names are not well known and arranging the fells in juxtaposition, area by area, tends to give a better semblance of order.

An index of fell names appears after the last chapter, on pages 270-271.

After the index, on pages 272-277, is a log of the walks for the use of readers.

At the end of the book is a note of the symbols used on the route maps.

Scout Scar

visiting
Cunswick Scar 679'
Scout Scar 764'

1000 feet of ascent

from KENDAL TOWN HALL
7½ miles
4 hours
but preferably
take sandwiches
and make a day of it

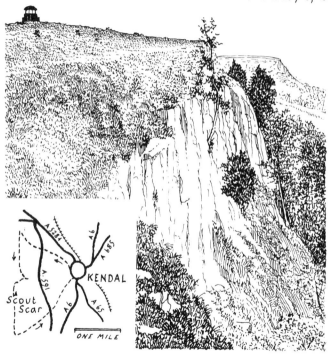

KENDAL

A591

A6
A684

A685

A6
A65

Scout
Scar

ONE MILE

The limestone escarpment that all local people
refer to as Scout Scar is named Underbarrow Scar
on Ordnance maps. Scout Scar properly is a much
smaller cliff to the south, not visited on this walk.

West of Kendal a sloping shelf of limestone rises at an easy gradient for two miles and then suddenly collapses in a long and spectacular cliff, the ground falling away sharply through a fringe of woodlands to the flat pastures of the Lyth Valley, once an inlet of the sea. The effect on the senses of this unexpected convulsion of the landscape is dramatic, even momentarily alarming on a first visit, and no matter how often repeated a slight feeling of shock returns each time as the scene is suddenly confronted. Coming up from Kendal there is nothing to suggest that the next step will not be like the last, but all at once you are on the brink of Scout Scar and ahead is a profound void.

But far below is a picture as fair as any in the country. Richly endowed with noble trees and emerald fields silvered by streams, the scattered white farmsteads of Lyth, renowned for their annual harvest of damsons, each in a surround of blossom, present a springtime scene with charm enough for a hundred canvasses, and in the other seasons of the year, even under snow, which comes but rarely to this sequestered sanctuary, the impression of rural tranquillity is one to lift the heart..... Even Kendal, a quiet country town, seems terribly urban in comparison.

Above this level strath a tangled array of colourful foothills rise inland from the estuary of the Kent against an exciting background: the hills of Lakeland, a rugged skyline of familiar summits, the mountains you once loved to climb. In other directions the panorama is even more extensive: the Howgill Fells are hardly less imposing, while Ingleborough and the Pennines fade into distance. As an all-round viewpoint Scout Scar ranks amongst the very best. Nothing is seen that is not beautiful. With one exception — Kendal's gas.holder.

The escarpment and the views are rewards enough, but the walk up from Kendal has merit too. It is on limestone, pure limestone without intrusions of other rocks, and is attended by the joys inherent in limestone: firm dry turf, here interspersed with gorse and juniper, heather and bracken; scree and clints that make tinkling music under the feet, and interesting formations, all allied to glorious views.

Scout Scar has a counterpart to the north, an almost identical twin, in Cunswick Scar: a mile-long, dead-straight escarpment, but curiously set back on another fault-line. In a fracture between the two is a scenic road with a popular car park.

This is a walk above others : a pleasure every step of the way.

3

In Serpentine Woods

This old summerhouse is passed during the walk through the woods. Note as you emerge on to the fell, in the wall between the gateway and the stile, a memorial tablet to DARWIN LEIGHTON "Friend of all creatures in this wood", whose daily ritual it was to feed the birds and squirrels. His name will be remembered by the older generation of fellwalkers as a member of the Fell and Rock Club.

Kendal Western Bypass as seen from the footbridge

At the end of the deep cutting the northbound motorist gets his first near view of the hills.

The cairn on Cunswick Scar, looking to Kentmere

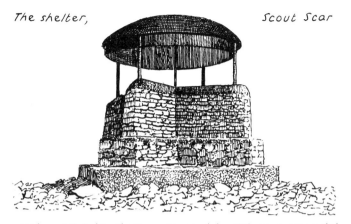

The shelter,   *Scout Scar*

This well-built shelter, erected in 1912 as a memorial to King George V and restored in 1969, is a conspicuous landmark on the highest part of Scout Scar. Formerly it was provided with a novel view indicator, which has been vandalised into extinction.

The Lakeland skyline from west to north

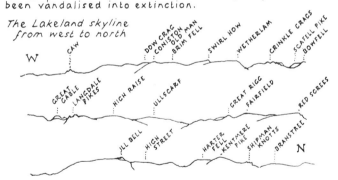

Ponder, as you walk upon Scout Scar: where does all the rain go that falls on this wide upland? The ground is bone dry. There are no streams. Does the rain simply percolate into the limestone and evaporate? Or is there, somewhere beneath the surface, a master cave, an underground lake with no outlet? Nowhere in the vicinity are there any resurgences, and there are no major springs.

The secret is locked in the twin bosoms of Cunswick Scar and Scout Scar. Man has, as yet, no key.

5

Leave Kendal's main street by way of Allhallows Lane (opposite the Town Hall) and the steep Beast Banks, where a handrail assists progress, turning from it into Serpentine Road to the entrance to Serpentine Woods on the left after 200 yards.   Enter this very delightful natural park (it is public and has a nature trail): there is a maze of paths amongst the trees but keep to the right and forward to a gateway and stile admitting to the open fell beyond, with a fine view suddenly revealed. Incline right to a clump of trees and there join a distinct track (a former quarry tramway) by a wall. Pass below Kettlewell Crag (the site of the quarry) and take a path rising to a stile in a wall-corner. Helsfell Nab is ahead; preferably walk over rather than under it, passing the 13th. tee of the golf course. The Nab is a neat little ridge, but not in the class of Striding Edge. Descend into the depression beyond and then rise sharply to the wall in front, where, to the right, is the first of a quick succession of five massive wooden step-stiles, which, with a footbridge, lead pedestrians across a new bypass road, opened in 1971, which at this point runs through a spectacular limestone ravine: a credit to the road engineers. Over the fifth stile the way is clear: a thin path rises gently over a large pasture containing the ruined target of a former rifle range, crosses a stile, and goes forward on open fell to the cairn on Cunswick Scar. After a breather descend to the edge of the escarpment and follow it to the left for a mile accompanied in the later stages by a wall and when this turns right go forward to a gate on the Underbarrow road. Go up the road for half a mile to a kissing gate on the left opposite a car park, whence a good path climbs to the unfenced escarpment of Scout Scar and a conspicuous circular shelter known locally as 'the umbrella' or 'the mushroom.'

▲ 679'

② stile

Cunswick Tarn

Cunswick Scar

③

old limekiln ✕

600

500   600

police mast ✕

UNDERBARROW 1¼

gate

④ car park

shelter and view indicator
▲ 764'

gate

600

shorter alternative route of return

Scout Scar

700

⑤ ▲

700

continuation opposite

continued ➞

6

MAP

ONE MILE

If a car is available the initial steep climb out of Kendal can be avoided by starting the walk at the top of the lane along the east side of Serpentine Woods.

WINDERMERE

Helsfell (farm)

rifle × target

barn

WINDERMERE

tee

Helsfell Nab stile

footbridge

①

Kettlewell Crag

barn

car park

BURNESIDE

river Kent

SHAP A6

Golf Course
600

Bus Station

Serpentine Woods

Town Hall

Kendal Western Road

Bank Head (farm)

quarries and lime works
500

Castle

river Kent

continuation opposite

Underbarrow Road A591

⑦

Fishers Tenement (farm)
500
600

cattle grid and gate

Brigsteer Road

Kendal

Church

By pass

racecourse

400

300

⑥

gate

LANCASTER

stile

500

BRIGSTEER

A6 LANCASTER

SETTLE A65

continued:
After a good long rest (no use overdoing things) depart from the shelter and resume the walk along the escarpment south for almost a mile until, in a slight depression, a path turns off left at a cairn and leads distinctly across open fell to a stile in a wall and a kissing gate in another (it seems a little nostalgic to be talking of kissing gates at our age) to cross a former racecourse and so reach the Brigsteer road at a cattle grid. An easy downhill mile along this, calling at the hospital for resuscitation if need be, will return you to Kendal Town Hall flushed with success.

Potter Fell

visiting
a nameless summit, 1262'
Brunt Knott, 1400'
a nameless summit, 1266'
Ulgraves, 1090'

1700 feet of ascent

*from THE BACK ROAD
between STAVELEY
and BOWSTON*

7½ miles

5 hours
but regard it
as a full-day
expedition.

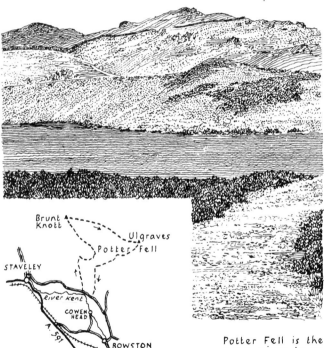

Potter Fell is the
name given to an
indefinite upland,
not to any summit
in particular.

The Lakes-bound motorist coming from the south is unlikely to pay much attention, if any at all, to the bracken-covered skyline in view on the right after Kendal is passed, being more intent on the scene unfolding ahead as greater mountains come into sight.

The bracken-covered skyline is that of Potter Fell. The motorist is right — it hardly merits more than a fleeting glance from the A.591 — but Potter Fell is not one to flaunt its charms. Charms it has, in plenty, but they are revealed only to those who go seeking them on foot.

Seen more intimately, the landscape is colourful and varied, with heather and bracken and mosses competing for ground space amidst grey rocks, but its special joy is a necklace of tarns, eight sheets of water being large enough to be so called, and of these the greatest in extent, Gurnal Dubs, is doubly endowed with an attractive setting and an island of trees.

The landscape is also confusing, a wild tangle of hillocks and shallow depressions, so that the line of march cannot be viewed far ahead, and were it not for identifiable walls on the map, route-finding would be difficult.

Occasionally a stray visitor may be met in the vicinity of Gurnal Dubs, but on the hills around never. North is a wilderness deeply enclosed by Kentmere and Longsleddale — a no-man's-wasteland. Therefore it behoves a walker subject to sudden maladies to endure a companion on this expedition, however solitary he may be by nature. You should choose a good-looker: you never know what might happen!

The cairn on Ulgraves

9

Side House

When the path from Side House comes abreast of this crag, turn left beyond it to reach the 1262' summit. Or, if you want to be a bit of a dare-devil, go straight up and over the rocks.

1 : Yoke
2 : Ill Bell
3 : Froswick
4 : Thornthwaite Crag

5 : The Knowe, Harter Fell
6 : Kentmere Pike
7 : Shipman Knotts

The summit of Brunt Knott

The tarns of Potter Fell

Most of the tarns on Potter Fell are reedy and shallow, with decorative names such as High, Low and Middle Taggleshaw that belie their relatively insignificant appearance when compared with the two largest (Gurnal Dubs and Potter Tarn), which, with another (Ghyll Pool), are used as reservoirs to supply the large paper mill of James Cropper & Co. Ltd. at Burneside, this firm having the exclusive water rights on the fell. Gurnal Dubs was originally two natural tarns (hence the plural name), formed into one by damming, but Potter Tarn is entirely artificial (as is evidenced by the walls running into and submerged by the water). Ghyll Pool is a smaller reservoir impounding a stream lower down the fellside and formerly supplied the village of Burneside also, but all three are now used for industrial purposes only.

Gurnal Dubs

A narrow country road
(commonly known as 'the
back road') connects
Staveley and Bowston,
and midway between
the two (1½ miles from
each), where the
River Kent comes
alongside, a lane
goes off north to
Side House (no signpost).
The walk starts here. There
is space to park a car
60 yards east of the junction.
Go up the lane, surfaced at first
but becoming rough, to the house,
pleasantly situated in a wooded
side-valley. Continue up the lane
past a small waterfall, reaching
the open fell half a mile further
at a gate and sheep pen. Here turn
right on a good track alongside a
wall, climbing steadily and
curving round to the north.
When the wall turns east
opposite a crag go left along
the line of a former wire fence
to an easy grass summit at 1262'
(no cairn). A thousand feet of
unremitting ascent has now been
completed and a rest well earned:
enjoy the fine view south over the
Kent Valley and west to Lakeland.
Brunt Knott is clearly seen ahead
in a patchwork of heather and bracken.
Follow a wall on the left down to a
depression, using a stile
in a crosswall there (note,
to the right, that this wall
curiously goes through the middle
of a large pool, which obviously has formed
since the wall was built). Now cross a path
and mount a steepening slope to the top of
Brunt Knott (Ordnance column S.5519), which
has a fine view of the valley heads of Kentmere
and Longsleddale. With two-thirds of the walk
still to be done do not tarry overlong here but
re-gird your ancient loins and aim east to a
junction of walls, crossing by a stile in the
corner (not easy: be careful) and climbing again, with a
wall on the left, to another unnamed summit (1266'; much
heather; no cairn). Keeping to the height of land, in the
same direction, proceed over sundry undulations, crossing
two walls at gaps used by sheep, to bring the abrupt top of
Ulgraves into view ahead across a depression. continued

BRUNT KNOTT
1400' n
1300
1200
1100
1000
STAVELEY
pool
stile
LONGSLEDDALE
1100
1200
stile
1262'
1100
gate and
sheep pen
1000
Birk Field
(farm)
Potter
Tarn
Frost
Hole
(farm)
800
gate
gate Side House
line of
aqueduct
700
600
STAVELEY 1½
High
Hundhowe
gates
River Kent
Hagg
Foot
(farm)
Cowen
Head
BOWSTON S
300

continuation opposite

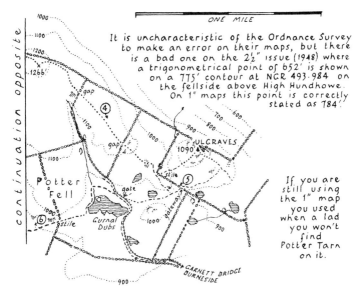

ONE MILE

It is uncharacteristic of the Ordnance Survey to make an error on their maps, but there is a bad one on the 2½" issue (1948) where a trigonometrical point of 652' is shown on a 775' contour at NGR 493.984 on the fellside above High Hundhowe. On 1" maps this point is correctly stated as 784'.

continuation opposite

If you are still using the 1" map you used when a lad you won't find Potter Tarn on it.

continued

Ulgraves looks a bit daunting across a sea of bracken and is further defended by a high wall, which is reached at a corner where there is an awkward stile calling for intense concentration; or an emaciated walker may try to insinuate himself through a sheep-crawl at this point (if both manœuvres are considered too fraught with peril follow the wall down to a wide gateway without a gate).

Ulgraves is a nice little climb and its tall cairn has a full-length view of Longsleddale. Descend to the gateway and cross a low ridge, passing a shallow tarn, to a gate in a wire fence. Gurnal Dubs is in front and is rounded by a lovely path on its north side. From the outlet go west over a low ridge (stile in wall) and forward down to Potter Tarn (dead-easy stile in wall). From the dam here a pleasant track leads downhill, passing a pool on the right and a reservoir on the left and descending alongside a wooded dell that is crossed by the Thirlmere aqueduct: note the iron gates and the bridge carrying the pipe over the beck. Lower, beyond a pumphouse, the track curves left and soon a gate on the right admits to a narrow bridleway leading to the road at the entrance to High Hundhowe, a lovely house.

If you parked a car, you can reasonably expect to find it a third of a mile west. If not, both Staveley and Bowston have bus services.

Green Quarter Fell

visiting
Hollow Moor, 1394'
a nameless summit, 1370'
with a detour to
Skeggles Water

1000 feet of ascent

from KENTMERE CHURCH

$4\frac{3}{4}$ miles

3 hours

(4 miles,
$2\frac{1}{2}$ hours,
omitting
the detour)

KENTMERE
GREEN
QUARTER
HOLLOW MOOR
Green
Quarter
Fell
Skeggles
Water

River Kent
Kentmere

ONE MILE

A.591
WINDERMERE
STAVELEY

Green Quarter Fell is the
foreground in this view,
not, alas, the background!

14

Green Quarter Fell is the featureless grassy height overlooking the hamlet of Kentmere to the east, and walkers in the valley invariably turn their backs on it and proceed to the fine surround of hills ahead, as indeed they should if they have youth on their side — for Green Quarter Fell has nothing to compare with the broad acres of High Street or the rough ridges leading thereto. Yet this modest fell, though rarely visited, has one thing the others lack — a perfectly-balanced and lovely view of upper Kentmere, best seen from the path used in descent, that cries aloud for a camera.

This apart, the long easy climb is without excitement and its accomplishment is gratifying only as evidence that there is life in the old dog yet.

The start of the bridleway

Skeggles Water from the bridleway

Skeggles Water, from Hollow Moor

Skeggles Water, lying in a vast bowl of heather, is conveniently visited on this walk but is an uninviting place with attractions mainly for bird-watchers and anglers. A few years ago a proposal to exploit the tarn for diatomite was defeated by concerted objections from local people and amenity societies.

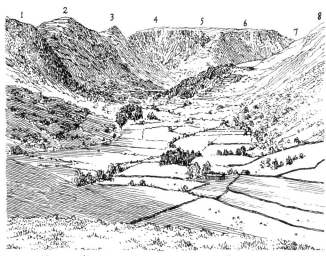

Upper Kentmere, as seen on the descent

1: Rainsborrow Crag   5: High Street
2: Ill Bell   6: Mardale Ill Bell
3: Froswick   7: Nan Bield Pass
4: Thornthwaite Crag   8: slopes of Harter Fell

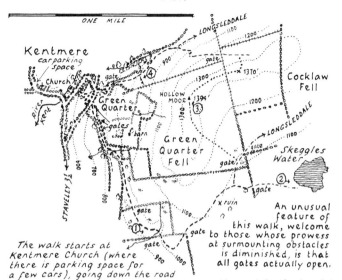

ONE MILE

Kentmere
car parking space
Church
River Kent
Green Quarter
gates
barn
STAVELEY 3½
LONGSLEDDALE
1100
1200
gate
900
1300
1370'
HOLLOW MOOR
1390'
1200
Cocklaw Fell
Green Quarter Fell
LONGSLEDDALE
1100
gate
Skeggles Water
gate
x ruin
gate
gate

An unusual feature of this walk, welcome to those whose prowess at surmounting obstacles is diminished, is that all gates actually open.

The walk starts at Kentmere Church (where there is parking space for a few cars), going down the road to Low Bridge and there turning up a side road to the hamlet of Green Quarter, cutting off a loop by a signposted footpath. Or, to avoid the steep pull up to Green Quarter, a car may be parked among the buildings there, with permission, or a walker may be dropped at this point for collection later.

Two signposts are prominent on the roadside here — one says 'Footpath to Longsleddale (Sadgill)' and is our route of return; the other, 100 yards south, says 'Bridleway to Longsleddale via Cocklaw Fell' and the outward route goes through a gate here (the first of many). The bridleway is initially unenclosed but soon runs between walls. When the wall on the left turns uphill take the branch path following it and cross a stream. Now the route is clearly defined for the next mile, the path climbing gradually and curving round the fellside in a wide loop to bring Skeggles Water into sight. Beyond a ruin the path bifurcates, the more obvious branch heading directly for a gate in a wall admitting to Skeggles Water, which may now be visited. Then resume the bridleway, leaving it after the next gate to ascend the easy grass slope half-left and so reach the top of the fell, which is adorned with a stone gatepost and has a superb view of the head of Kentmere. Continue by curving east along the ridge to a cross-fence, simply negotiated by cocking one leg over and then the other. Just beyond, in tussocky grass, is a secondary summit (no cairn), from which descend the north slope to join an old cart-track that goes down gently to Green Quarter. Take your time along this easy terrace and enjoy one of the most beautiful views in Lakeland.

High Knott

better known as
Williamson's Monument
901'

with a detour to
the Village Settlement
at Hugill

620 feet of ascent

from BROWFOOT,
KENTMERE

5 miles

3 hours

This fine cairn on High Knott
incorporates a tablet with the
following inscription:

In Memory of
THOMAS WILLIAMSON
of Height, in Hugil, Gent.
who died Feb. 13th 1797
Aged 66 years.
Erected 1803

Heights is the nearest farm in
view southwest. The cairn was
built by the Rev. T. Williamson
in memory of his father, who
used to climb up to High Knott
every day before breakfast.

18

High Knott is an abrupt knoll not greatly elevated above the general level of the green fell from which it rises but occupying a strategic position with a commanding oversight of the loveliest part of the Kentmere valley.   The British Settlement a mile distant is a site of some significance historically but although the earthworks are fairly distinct the imagination of the layman is no substitute for the trained eye of the archaeologist and the unlearned visitor is likely to be disappointed with the scanty remains.   The charm of this outing, for the walker pure and simple (if such a creature there be), lies rather in following old bridleways, today virtually unused, over the pleasant heights on the west side of mid-Kentmere.

The British Settlement at Hugill

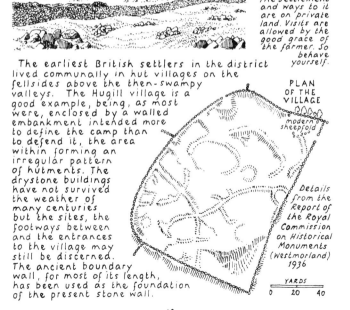

The Settlement and ways to it are on private land. Visits are allowed by the good grace of the farmer. So behave yourself.

The earliest British settlers in the district lived communally in hut villages on the fellsides above the then-swampy valleys.   The Hugill village is a good example, being, as most were, enclosed by a walled embankment intended more to define the camp than to defend it, the area within forming an irregular pattern of hutments. The drystone buildings have not survived the weather of many centuries but the sites, the footways between and the entrances to the village may still be discerned. The ancient boundary wall, for most of its length, has been used as the foundation of the present stone wall.

PLAN OF THE VILLAGE

modern sheepfold

Details from the Report of the Royal Commission on Historical Monuments (Westmorland) 1936

YARDS
0   20   40

19

Ulthwaite Bridge dates from the 17th century and is scheduled as an historical monument. Ordnance maps spell the name *Ulthwaite*.

Arrange transport to and from Browfoot (on the by-road west of the River Kent) to save four miles of road-walking from and to Staveley. (Or the walk could as conveniently start and finish at Ulthwaite Bridge off the main valley road).

Go up the tarmac road west of Browfoot and enter the first gate on the left. A public path ascends two fields and meets an impasse in the top corner of the second (no stile or gate or sheep-crawl): use the wall-corner as a stile (fairly easy, but mind your dentures don't drop out). Then cross southwards over the next field to an unusual stile near a wall-corner and from it ascend left to the fine memorial cairn on High Knott, a good vantage point with a distant view of Lakeland's fells and an intimate one of mid-Kentmere. Return to the stile and use a gate on the left into the Hugill lane, which follow to the right until its enclosing walls end at gates. From this point the British settlement is two fields forward, through another gate, and located near a clump of trees. Return to the end of the lane and use the next gate to follow a rutted bridleway north until a gate on the right leads into a pasture threaded by Park Beck, the path becoming lost in wet ground. Do not cross the stream but follow it down until, at a larch, a path fords it. Take this path: it enters a large field, goes across it indistinctly to a gate, beyond which is a small stone cottage used only by sheep, and then descends clearly amid bracken and trees to a walled lane passing Croft Head and emerging at Ulthwaite Bridge, which do not cross, keeping along a pleasant riverside lane to Browfoot.

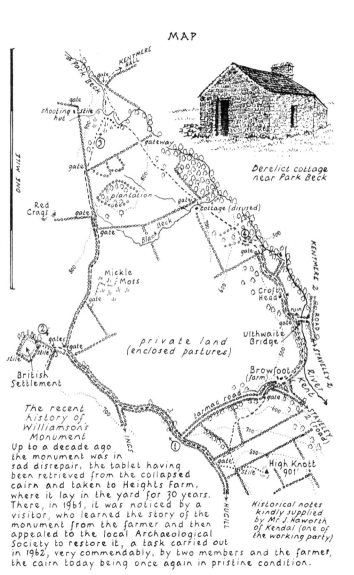

KENTMERE HALL

Park Beck

gate

gate

shooting hut · stile

500

③

gateway

gate

plantation

Red Crags

gate

gate

Black Beck

800

cottage (disused)

gate

700

④

500

KENTMERE 2

gate

600

Croft Head

ruin

gate

ONE MILE

Mickle Moss

gate

Ulthwaite Bridge

500

Derelict cottage near Park Beck

② gates
gate

stile stile

British Settlement

private land
(enclosed pastures)

700

Browfoot (farm)

Kent River

tarmac road

gate

600

STAVELEY 2

gate

STAVELEY 2 (road)

KENTMERE 2 ROAD → STAVELEY 2

①

700

gate

stile

800

High Knott
901 ▲

INGS

HUGILL

The recent history of Williamson's Monument

Up to a decade ago the monument was in sad disrepair, the tablet having been retrieved from the collapsed cairn and taken to Heights Farm, where it lay in the yard for 30 years. There, in 1961, it was noticed by a visitor, who learned the story of the monument from the farmer and then appealed to the local Archaeological Society to restore it, a task carried out in 1962, very commendably, by two members and the farmer, the cairn today being once again in pristine condition.

Historical notes kindly supplied by Mr J. Haworth of Kendal (one of the working party)

21

Hugill Fell
840'
530 feet of ascent

from STAVELEY

1 mile up and
1 mile down by
the same route

1½ hours

CRINKLE CRAGS
SCAFELL
SCAFELL PIKE
BOWFELL
GREAT END
ALLEN CRAGS
LOFT CRAG
GREAT GABLE
HARRISON STICKLE

KENTMERE
KENTMERE
Hugill
Fell
WINDERMERE — BOWSTON
STAVELEY
River
Kent
CROOK
A 591
KENDAL

ONE MILE

Hugill Fell, the low ridge on
the west side of the Kentmere
valley just out of Staveley, is
patterned by stone walls that
restrict free wandering. One
route only is practicable: this
fortunately leads to the finest
viewpoint on the fell, marked
by a prominent cairn, directly
overlooking the valley, with a
good prospect of the mountains
of Lakeland and a panorama
ranging as far as Ingleborough.
   The climb to it is short and
sweet but initially steep.

22

MAP

Take the Kentmere road from Staveley for half a mile until, on the left, immediately beyond a stream coming down the fellside, an iron gate near a hen-hut gives access to a track climbing steeply past a bungalow ("Hillside").

Keep to the track past mature larches until it fades as the slope eases. A wall is now seen on the right: aim for its top corner, rounding it to reach the cairn. Return the same way.

Can a traverse be made to the nearby summits of Reston Scar and High Knott? NO, nor to either one of them. High and collapsable drystone walls prevent this. Gates are few, and no key to a through route. Finding a legitimate way amongst the network of walls is like trying to solve a bent-nail puzzle, except that in this case there is positively no solution. Each of the three summits has its own permissible access but no communication with the other two.

The Kentmere Valley, from Hugill Fell

23

Reston Scar
834'
520 feet of ascent

from STAVELEY

1 mile up and
1 mile down by
the same route

1½ hours

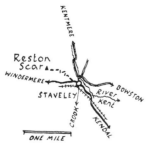

Reston
Scar

WINDERMERE

STAVELEY

KENTMERE

BOWSTON

River
Kent

CROOK

KENDAL

ONE MILE

There must be many readers who, like the author, have been passing Reston Scar en route for the Lakes with no more than a glance up at it, regularly for donkeys years. Now it offers a consolation prize. The climb is steep but a good cart-track eases the gradient and continues almost to the cairn. This is a fine place for a siesta on a sunny day (with a tarn to paddle in) while the rest of the family go on to Helvellyn.

MAP

Leave Staveley village centre by the Kentmere road, and use the first lane on the left to reach the 'top' road, where, 50 yards to the left, a gated lane turns up the fellside to serve two houses. Beyond, it continues distinctly as a rutted cart-track, ascending the steep slope in a series of loops, passing first through a gate near a covered reservoir and then another bearing a faded notice that says something about a bull, this gate being followed by a third in 15 yards from which the track traverses the easy top of Reston Scar, ending at a gated wall where the cairn is only a minute away on the left. From here Hugill Fell and High Knott to the north appear to offer a pleasant extension of the walk, but impassable walls bar the way and there is no alternative but to return to Staveley by the route of ascent.

looking north from Reston Scar

Orrest Head

783'

400 feet of ascent

from WINDERMERE
RAILWAY STATION
2½ miles
2 hours
by the route described
1 mile : 1 hour
there and back direct

from the north

Orrest Head, for many of us, is "where we came in" — our first ascent in Lakeland, our first sight of mountains in tumultuous array across glittering waters, our awakening to beauty. It is a popular walk, deservedly, for here the promised land is seen in all its glory. It is a fitting finale, too, to a life made happy by fellwandering. Dare we hope there will be another Orrest Head over the threshold of the next heaven?

The way to Orrest Head is announced by a large signboard, which proclaims its unrivalled views and states that it is a twenty minutes' walk to the top. It is the leftmost of three drives that leave the main road near the bus stops opposite the railway station, and is a tarmac strip initially. Almost at once a footpath goes off to the left: ignore this, keeping ahead and climbing gradually in a series of loops and bends. When a farm is reached the path becomes rough; further, it divides into three branches: take the one on the right by a wall to reach and enter a fenced lane with many seats. This leads to a kissing gate; in the wall alongside is a memorial tablet to Arthur Henry Heywood, whose family gave Orrest Head for public enjoyment. Through the gate, and clear of trees at last, the view-indicator on the summit is seen on the left and soon reached. There is a choice of seats — iron, wood, stone and grass — from which to admire the fine view and reflect that, once upon a time, you could have done this climb in twenty minutes just like that signboard said. Never mind. You've had a good innings.

Return the same way, or, if a longer alternative route is preferred, leave the rocky top by a path heading north to a quiet byroad, which follow left to join the A.592 road (to Troutbeck) but without actually setting foot on it go through a gate on the left (public footpath sign), whence a good path leads forward into a wood and continues very pleasantly past some handsome residences amid noble trees, rejoining the outward route only a few paces from the starting point: in fact along the path ignored earlier.

There is a plan afoot to re-align the A.591 through the woods below Orrest. If this comes to pass, (which heaven forfend!) the start and finish of this walk will also need re-routing.

MAP

HALF A MILE

The view indicator on the summit

Windermere

THE VIEW

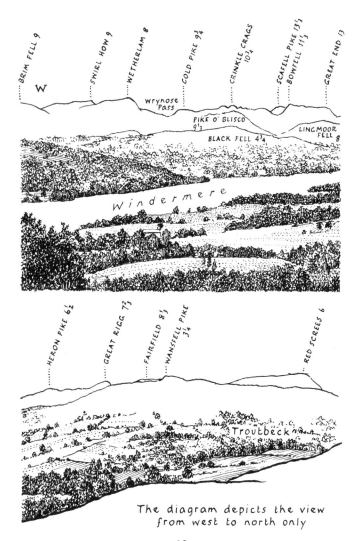

BRIM FELL 9

W

SWIRL HOW 9

WETHERLAM 8

COLD PIKE 9¾

CRINKLE CRAGS 10¼

SCAFELL PIKE 13⅓

BOWFELL 11⅓

GREAT END 13

Wrynose Pass

PIKE O' BLISCO 9⅓

BLACK FELL 4¾

LINGMOOR FELL 8

Windermere

HERON PIKE 6½

GREAT RIGG 7⅓

FAIRFIELD 8⅓

WANSFELL PIKE 3¼

RED SCREES 6

Troutbeck

The diagram depicts the view
from west to north only

THE VIEW

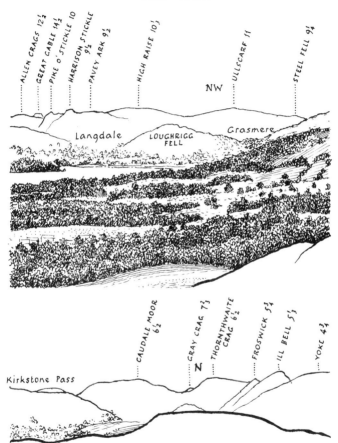

The thick line is the outline of the summit rocks.

The figures accompanying the names of fells
indicate distances in miles.

Summit seats and litter, which occur in profusion,
and the view indicator, are omitted.

School Knott

visiting
  School Knott, 760'
  Grandsire, 818'
  a nameless summit, 806'

700 feet of ascent

*from WINDERMERE
RAILWAY STATION*
**5 miles
2½ hours**

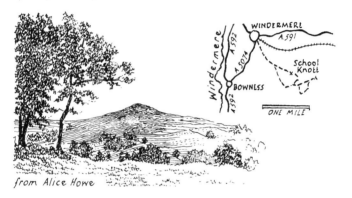

from Alice Howe

School Knott is the bare fell rising southeast of Windermere Railway Station and giving the finest view of the town: a splendid prospect backed by the lake and the mountains around Langdale.   It is a favourite playground for the youngsters from the new housing estate at its base and a gentle excursion for the older residents and visitors whose mountain days are a dim memory.   Surprisingly for so popular a climb its grassy top has no cairn.   In a fold of the hills behind is, unexpectedly, a large tarn, and beyond this is another fell, Grandsire, similar in height but very different in character: a rough little wilderness of heather and bracken and bog, rarely visited yet a more enchanting place to while away a sunny hour.

Approaches to School Knott have been changed, the building of the Droomer Estate having cut into the old pleasant byway between Alice Howe and Cleabarrow at the foot of the fell. Access is now gained at the points indicated on the map opposite.

30

MAP

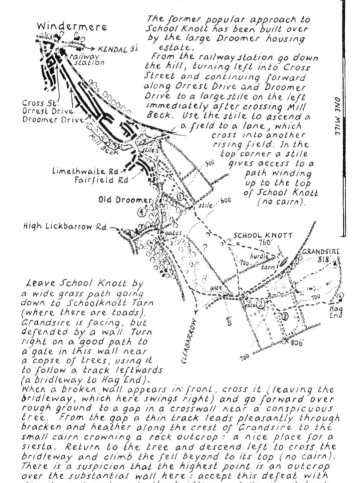

The former popular approach to School Knott has been built over by the large Droomer housing estate.

From the railway station go down the hill, turning left into Cross Street and continuing forward along Orrest Drive and Droomer Drive to a large stile on the left immediately after crossing Mill Beck. Use the stile to ascend a field to a lane, which cross into another rising field. In the top corner a stile gives access to a path winding up to the top of School Knott (no cairn).

Windermere
← KENDAL 8½
railway station

Cross St.
Orrest Drive
Droomer Drive

Mill Beck

stile

Limethwaite Rd
Fairfield Rd

Old Droomer

stile 600

High Lickbarrow Rd

gates

SCHOOL KNOTT
760'

hurdle
tarn

GRANDSIRE
818'

gate

Hag End

CLEABARROW

806'

ONE MILE

Leave School Knott by a wide grass path going down to Schoolknott Tarn (where there are toads). Grandsire is facing, but defended by a wall. Turn right on a good path to a gate in this wall near a copse of trees, using it to follow a track leftwards (a bridleway to Hag End).

When a broken wall appears in front, cross it (leaving the bridleway, which here swings right) and go forward over rough ground to a gap in a crosswall near a conspicuous tree. From the gap a thin track leads pleasantly through bracken and heather along the crest of Grandsire to the small cairn crowning a rock outcrop: a nice place for a siesta. Return to the tree and descend left to cross the bridleway and climb the fell beyond to its top (no cairn). There is a suspicion that the highest point is an outcrop over the substantial wall here: accept this defeat with dignity and go down to the bridleway, following it back to the copse and there turn left, through a gate, on a charming path descending to join an unenclosed lane, which goes north to pass Old Droomer and join, beyond, the outward route above the housing estate.

31

Old Droomer

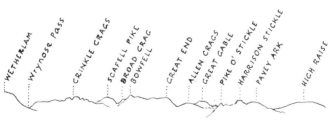

WETHERLAM · WRYNOSE PASS · CRINKLE CRAGS · SCAFELL PIKE · **BROAD CRAG** BOWFELL · GREAT END · ALLEN CRAGS · GREAT GABLE · PIKE O' STICKLE · HARRISON STICKLE · PAVEY ARK · HIGH RAISE

Four sections of Windermere (lake) are in view
from the top of School Knott. If you can
spot them all your eyes aren't
as bad as you feared.

Windermere

Windermere
(town)

The Langdale skyline, from School Knott

Summit outcrop, School Knott

Summit outcrop, Grandsire

Grandsire and Schoolknott Tarn

Brant Fell
629'
450 feet of ascent

from Post Knott

Summit rocks

A visitor to Bowness with time to kill, or wishing to escape from the throngs of day-trippers, cannot do better than walk up Brant Fell and, in solitude, enjoy its fine prospect of Windermere or a simple scramble on its inviting summit rocks. Old-timers will remember that the top was once adorned with a building, of which only a few relics now remain. The fell is privately owned but open to the public through the good grace of the owner.

34

ONE MILE

AMBLESIDE 5
A 592

WINDERMERE I
A 5074

Windermere

Church

Bowness

Biskey
Howe

Helm Road

gas
holders

MANSION
GROUND

gate

Brantfell
Road

KENDAL 8½
A 592

NEWBY BRIDGE 7
A 592

gate 400

gate

farm
road

Post
Knott

Brantfell
Farm

reservoir

gap

BRANT FELL
629'

Brantfell Road rises sharply from the
streets of Bowness near to St. Martin's
Church and at its upper end a
footpath continues in the same
direction through fields. Turn
off this to the right after the
second crosswall and enter
a woodland by a broad
fenced path that leads
to a stile giving access to
the viewpoint, Post Knott.
From here Brant Fell
is clearly in sight,
and there seems to
be no objection to a
beeline, crossing a
trodden-down wall in
the hollow between: a
popular trespass. On
the top of Brant Fell, a
fine viewpoint, occur the
railings, foundations and a well of a former summerhouse, which
was destroyed in a fire, and there are some good rock scrambles.
  Descend north to reach a cart-track near a small reservoir, and
follow this left through the yard of Brantfell Farm, turning left
from the farm road beyond into a lane and field, so rejoining the
outward route above Brantfell Road. At this point the return can
be varied by entering the gated woodland path on the right and
so reaching Helm Road, where, on the right, steps lead up to the
rocky knoll of Biskey Howe. Then go down Helm Road to Bowness.

The lower reaches of Windermere

Whitbarrow

visiting
Lord's Seat 706'

800 feet of ascent

from MILL SIDE,
WITHERSLACK
6½ miles
4 hours

Mill Side

36

Whitbarrow is an abrupt ridge of limestone on a north-south axis soaring boldly above the flat marshes and mosses of the Kent Estuary and is a parallel counterpart to the long cliff of Scout Scar across the alluvial valley of Lyth. Rich woodlands clothe the lower slopes and in the east pine plantations climb almost to the summit. To the west a four-mile escarpment extends along the crest like a castle wall and is repeated on a smaller scale at the highest limits of the eastern forests. But the spine of the ridge is bare, although 'bare' is an inapt word for the wealth of heather and bracken, juniper and saplings that form so colourful a carpet. In places this carpet has worn thin, revealing a naked surface of patchy scree and outcrops of dazzling whiteness.

Whitbarrow's delights of plant and wild life have been recognised by the recent adoption of its summit plateau as a nature reserve, and there is nowhere a more attractive landscape in which to enjoy the manifold pleasures of a natural environment allied to a far-reaching and very lovely panorama.

The walk described is the most beautiful in this book; beautiful it is every step of the way. It includes a traverse of the finest part of the scar top and returns through delightful woods along the base of the cliffs. After initial steepness the walking is exceedingly pleasant, in surroundings high above encircling valleys and amidst scenery that has no blemish. All is fair to the eye on Whitbarrow.

looking north
to Lord's Seat

The Nature Reserve

The Lake District Naturalists' Trust was formed in 1962 largely as a result of the efforts of Canon G.A.K. Hervey, and after his death in 1967 an inspired proposal to acquire Flodder Allotment (the walled enclosure including Lord's Seat on the highest part of Whitbarrow) as a memorial to him was happily brought to fruition. The area was declared a nature reserve in 1969, a visible recognition of the Canon's services to the Trust being accorded by a tablet built into a fine new cairn on Lord's Seat and inscribed as follows:

This Reserve
Commemorates
CANON G.A.K. HERVEY
1893-1967
Founder of the
Lake District Naturalists' Trust

The emblem of the Trust

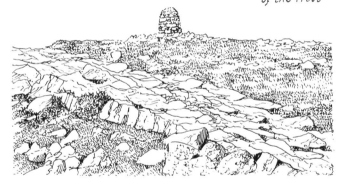

Lonely Whitbarrow, remote from urban influences, is the last place one would associate with industrial exploitation, and it is strange to find in a corner of Flodder Allotment the scanty but obvious remains of a drift mine, with an open level still penetrating deep into the fellside — the sort of place readers of this book would have enjoyed exploring in their heyday, but not now.

The nature of the spoil suggests that iron was extracted.

Chapel Head
Scar

Beck Head

39

Mill Side is an outpost of Witherslack a third of a mile off the Grange-Levens Bridge road (A.590), and is a pleasant hamlet with a mill dam, now attractively incorporated in a private garden. From the dam take the uphill road past a farmhouse, heading for the vertical end of Whitbarrow Scar, which dominates this rural scene. At the top of the road turn right along a lane and, when buildings come into sight ahead, ascend a thin path branching left into the woodland until a stream is reached. At this point exactly, turn sharp left on a higher path above the line of approach to a gap in a wall on the top of the Scar. (By trending more to the left through the trees before reaching the gap, Whitbarrow Cave will be found at the base of the vertical cliff — the traverse to it is perilous for old men with brittle limbs and the detour is not really worth the bother, the cave being only 15' long). The gap is immediately succeeded by another on the right, so giving access to the open fell. Climbing gradually, a broken wall is crossed to a cairned summit, from which point the full length of the traverse of the scar top to the furthest cairn in sight, on Lord's Seat, can be surveyed. Go forward over an intermediate summit (large cairn), keeping near to a fenced pine plantation on the right, and continue to a gap in a cross-wall ahead, where a path will be found leading onwards along the base of a continuous escarpment on the right, the delightful surroundings being akin to a natural rock garden. When the cairn on Lord's Seat appears within close range leave the path and head straight for it (first, if desired, detouring to a charming pool, unseen but found in a hollow 100 yards to the right).   Lord's Seat is centred in an interesting limestone landscape and has good distant views. Rest awhile here, keeping your chest well covered up if there is a breeze, and then proceed north to a cross-wall, where turn left on a path passing near an old mine-level and then descending sharply on the fringe of a scree slope to a stile in another wall, where a sign of the Lake District Naturalists' Trust is affixed. The path goes roughly into the wood, becoming easier at the foot of the slope. Ignore paths branching left and right and go on ahead through the wood, the path becoming a cart-track before emerging on a tarmac road. Turn left along this quiet road, a lovely avenue of trees, getting a splendid glimpse of the stately pile of Witherslack Hall. A farm on the left is passed, and at the bottom of the short hill beyond (adjoining the main entrance-drive to the Hall), turn left along a lane, passing farm buildings, into an open field with the very impressive cliffs of Chapel Head Scar ahead. Cross the field, bearing slightly left, to a gate on the edge of the wood below the cliffs. Through it, turn right on a wide path amidst trees for a full mile to emerge on a lane near Beck Head, which, followed to the left, returns you to Mill Side. The final delight of the route is the remarkable resurgence at the base of a low cliff by the roadside that gives the lovely hamlet of Beck Head its name.

This walk should not be done in the reverse direction: there might be trouble in locating the way off the Scar.

MAP

The full route as described opposite may be overlong for octogenarians and upwards, who, instead, may make two shorter walks out of it:

A:
from WITHERSLACK HALL
3½ miles

From the road at the entrance-drive to the Hall, go across the open field east to a gate on the edge of the wood. Here take a path to the left for 300 yards, where a cairn indicates a rough track branching up to a gap in a wall. Continue in the same direction (no path) to Lord's Seat, joining the full route to return past the old mine and down to the road north of the Hall.

B:
from MILL SIDE:
5 miles

Use the full route as far as Lord's Seat, where turn down south-south-west (no path) to a made gap in the scar wall with a LDNT sign affixed on the far side: it is essential to find and identify this gap, which marks the only breach in the cliffs. From it a rough track descends half-left amongst trees to the foot of the slope, joining a better path that, followed left for 300 yards, reaches a gate where the full route is joined for the return via Beck Head to Mill Side.

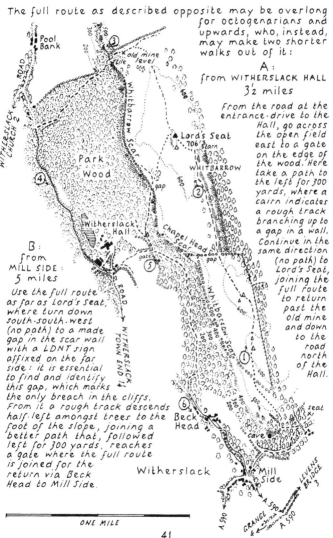

ONE MILE

41

Cartmel Fell

(Raven's Barrow, 500')

300 feet of ascent

FROM
CARTMEL FELL CHURCH
1¾ miles
1 hour

The Winster valley, having survived a threat of death by drowning, continues to delight visitors with its rural tranquillity and charm, the scene being best surveyed from the elevated tangle of bracken and coppice forming its western flanks. This is Cartmel Fell. Much of it is privately owned and decoratively laid out with plantations and artificial tarns, but the part overlooking the ancient church is accessible and offers a short and pleasant ramble. A conspicuous cairn here might have looked down on a sterile reservoir but for a spirited opposition; happily it is still a lovely belvedere for viewing a lovely valley.

St Anthony's Church, probably a foundation of Cartmel Priory, has several interesting and unusual features. It is not easy to locate in a labyrinth of quiet lanes but the reward is worth the search.

Cairn on Raven's Barrow locally known as Ravensbarrow (or Rainsbarrow) Old Man.

42

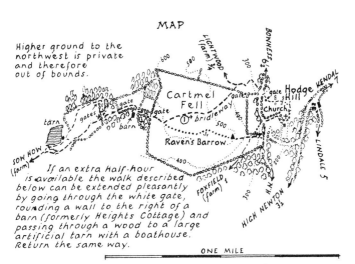

MAP

Higher ground to the northwest is private and therefore out of bounds.

Cartmel Fell
① bridleway
Raven's Barrow

If an extra half-hour is available the walk described below can be extended pleasantly by going through the white gate, rounding a wall to the right of a barn (formerly Heights Cottage) and passing through a wood to a large artificial tarn with a boathouse. Return the same way.

ONE MILE

This is a walk too good to be omitted, yet it is short and confined to a single walled enclosure on Cartmel Fell known as Raven's Barrow. It is, in fact, ideal for filling in an hour while the rest of the family are inspecting the quaint church or attending service there.   Excusing yourself from their company, go round the churchyard wall left of the lychgate and follow a path ascending by another wall amongst trees and bracken to a road junction where, directly opposite, a footpath sign points to Foxfield, 1 mile.   Go over the stile here and climb half-left (no visible path) to another stile in a wall above a holly tree. Over it, join a path going straight up to the well-built monolithic cairn prominent above, which commands a fine view of the lovely Winster valley. Wander west across the open top, descending slightly, to a white gate near a plantation. From this, a good bridleway leads back to the road crossed earlier at a point where a facing gate and field paths give a variation return route to the church.

St Anthony's Church.
Cartmel Fell

43

Gummer's How
1054'

390 feet of ascent

from THE NEWBY BRIDGE TO
BOWLAND BRIDGE ROAD

1 mile there and back
1 hour plus

The time comes to every Lakeland fellwalker, in due course, when he has good reason to give thanks to Gummer's How for salvaging his pride. Here is a fellwalk in miniature, a little beauty, with heather, a few rocks to scramble on, soft couches for repose, a classic view and a rustic Ordnance column ——— just like the real thing; and all so easy of access from a motor road and attainable almost without effort. White hair and Gummer's How are akin. It is an old man's mountain. And when ancient legs can no longer climb it know ye that the sad day has come to hang up the boots for ever and take to slippers.

MAP

No written description of the ascent is given.

Let this be a test of map reading, route finding and direction sense. If these abilities are so diminished that you get lost the future for you is bleak and without hope.

The initial stile is the only hazard.

On the summit, take a path going northwest of the column (100 yards) for the best view of Windermere.

Apart from summit variations there is no alternative route of return to the road. Be careful getting back over the stile.

HALF A MILE

GUMMER'S HOW 1054'

800
900
700

stile

BOWLAND BRIDGE 2

ROAD

NEWBY BRIDGE 1½

roadside parking for several cars

Gummer's How from Lake Side

SWAN

The diagram shows the major Lakeland fells in view from the summit. Additionally, to the east, the Howgills and the Pennine skyline can be seen. South is Morecambe Bay and the estuaries of the Kent and Crake.

The highlight of the panorama is the fine full-length prospect of Windermere, seen best from a vantage point northwest of the Ordnance column. Esthwaite Water also displays its full length but is greatly foreshortened by distance.

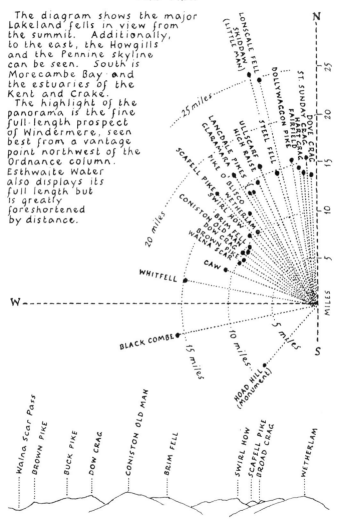

looking northwest to the Coniston Fells

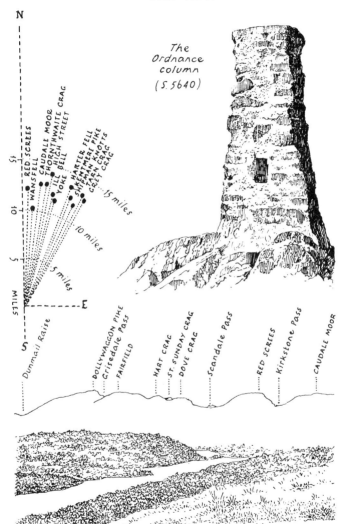

The
Ordnance
column
(S. 5640)

N

RED SCREES
WANSFELL
CAUDALE MOOR
THORNTHWAITE CRAG
ILL BELL
HIGH STREET
YOKE
HARTER FELL
KENTMERE PIKE
SHIPMAN KNOTTS
CROWN KNOTTS
GREEN CRAG

15

10

5

MILES

15 miles

10 miles

5 miles

E

Dunmail Raise

DOLLYWAGGON PIKE
GRISEDALE PASS
FAIRFIELD

HART CRAG
ST. SUNDAY CRAG
DOVE CRAG

Scandale Pass

RED SCREES

Kirkstone Pass

CAUDALE MOOR

looking north to the head of Windermere

47

Staveley Fell
870'
750 feet of ascent

from STAVELEY
IN FURNESS

3 miles
2 hours

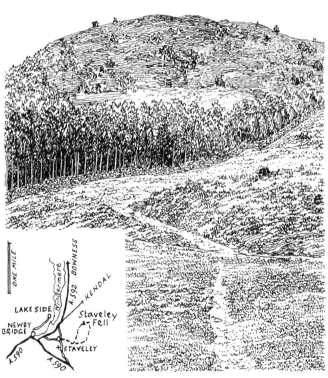

'Staveley Fell' is an adopted name for the high tract of ground overlooking the quiet hamlet of Staveley (in Furness; not the Westmorland one) and linking Gummer's How with Newton Fell in an uninterrupted ridge. Strictly it has no name, not even locally, being referred to on Ordnance maps as Astley's and Chapel House Plantations, which are new forests severely encroaching upon it. As yet the top of the fell has not been planted (not out of consideration for walkers but because the ground is too rocky and windswept); it is entirely encircled by new trees, however, so that within a few years it will be sealed off and inaccessible, unless the Forestry Commission, who have shown more tolerance for pedestrians latterly, provide a waymarked route through. This they are urged to do, if only to prevent damage to young trees, because the summit ridge is pleasantly attractive and appears so in the eyes of visitors down in the valley, and although not crossed by a right of way has hitherto had open access, a time-honoured privilege that should not be denied for the sake of a few more spruce. If no route is waymarked (this need be done only for a distance no greater than 300 yards) then the top of the fell will soon become a write-off for peakbaggers.   Which would be a pity, for it commands a fine aerial view of the foot of Windermere.

Staveley Church

49

The first cairn, looking to the highest summit (·x·)

The cairn on the highest summit, looking north to Gummer's How.

Staveley Fell provides a delightful short walk by the route indicated opposite, BUT bear in mind that it crosses Forestry Commission land and there is no evidence that intruders are welcome (in fact, one gets a contrary impression) AND that, apart from a thicket of trees, there are obstacles to progress in the form of dense bracken and rough deep heather (handicaps even in winter), so that unless you can bend your legs in all directions not excluding the ridiculous, and without warning, Staveley Fell is, alas, not for you.

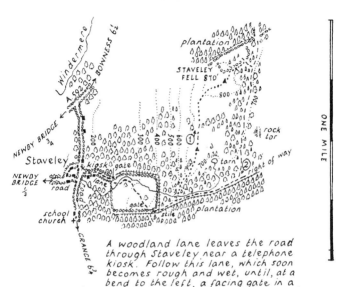

A woodland lane leaves the road
through Staveley near a telephone
kiosk. Follow this lane, which soon
becomes rough and wet, until, at a
bend to the left, a facing gate in a
wall admits to a large open enclosure. A cart track,
becoming a groove, crosses a stream and works round to
the left before bearing right, uphill, to a gate in the wall
bounding a large plantation on the south side. Through the
gate, ignore a high stile facing and turn left by the wall
to a slippery stile, needing care, in the forest fence. An
unenclosed path (a right of way) ascends beyond it. Our
objective is now half-left but new plantings among older
trees make both a beeline and a choice of route difficult
(no path), but 250 yards along the right of way it is just
possible to turn off and proceed without damaging young
trees (at the time of writing) and so reach a rocky ridge
above the planting line. The first cairned top is not the
highest — across a depression thick with bracken rise two
other summits, the nearest crowned with trees, the second
bare, with a cairn, and the highest point on the fell. From
this latter descend roughly north to an old wall just below
and follow it down to the right, meeting young trees again,
and, at a depression, turn down an unplanted avenue, on
the right, to join a forest path, none too clear, contouring
the slope. Follow this to the right for a long half-mile to
join the right of way, which can then be used to return to
Staveley, finishing the walk by the outward route.

THIS WALK IS RECOMMENDED ONLY WITH CERTAIN RESERVATIONS !!!!
(see note opposite)

Newton Fell

Travellers on the A.590 road between Lindale and Barrow Banks cannot fail to be aware of the steep and colourful ridge accompanying their passage on the east side, and fellwalkers (especially ancient ones) will eye it with favour: although not high its undulating skyline promises an interesting ramble. Unfortunately there are few points of access and the traverse of the whole ridge from end to end is not possible without trespass: parts of it are walled pastures and one promising approach is sealed off by reservoirs. A country road (High Newton to the Winster valley) crosses the ridge midway but cannot be left on foot, and only one right of way exists in the four-mile length of the fell.

Two features in particular will be noticed: the crag of White Stone rising steeply out of the bracken at its base, and the strange ruin on the skyline above Eller How. These, and adjacent sections of the ridge, may be visited in separate walks, by courtesy of the owners and tenants, as directed on pages 55 and 57.

The ridge is Newton Fell.

It is convenient to describe it in two parts: north and south of the country road bisecting it.

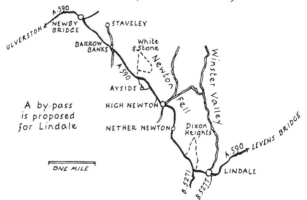

A by-pass is proposed for Lindale

ONE MILE

Newton Fell, from Barrow Banks

Newton Fell, above Eller How

The highest point of Newton Fell

The upper rocks
of White Stone

MAP
Newton Fell
(NORTH)

780'

600 feet of ascent

1¾ miles

1½ hours

FROM
WHITESTONE
CARAVAN SITE

ONE MILE

All the area shown on the map above east of the A.590 is privately owned and without public rights of way.

Yet White Stone is so appealing! It can, moreover, be reached from a good track leaving an iron gate on the roadside directly below — but not, alas, with an easy conscience. So it is better to seek permission from the friendly owner of the Whitestone Caravan Site to walk to it by using the paths climbing the fellside above the caravans: by so doing a circular route is possible.

Assuming permission—

From the 'crossroads' on the caravan site use a grassy path rising steadily to the right, and when this loops to the left continue up the fell to the substantial ridgewall, over which, unmarked by cairn or column, is the unattractive highest point of Newton Fell. Do not attempt to climb the wall (here the game is not worth the candle) but follow it left across two small depressions to a junction of walls, where a gap admits to the White Stone enclosure. There is no cairn here either and interest is confined to a cautious study of the crags from above. Then return to the gap and turn downhill to find a good path that descends directly to the caravan site across a colourful slope of bracken and outcropping rock, the lower parts being wooded with native trees, giving a pleasant finish.

55

The ruined tower on the top of Dixon Heights

The top of Dixon Heights is adorned with the remains of a substantial tower, conspicuous from afar but now only a shadow of its former self because of the operations of latter-day vandals, an inner chamber having been choked with stones torn from the fabric although habitable and used by the Home Guard during the last war. The origins and purpose of the tower are obscure. There is a legend that it was a lookout for the observation of smugglers in the estuary but it seems equally likely to have been merely a decoration of the Eller How estate, this theory being supported by the presence of other ornamental stonework in the vicinity.

In view from Dixon Heights is Helton Tarn in the Winster valley, which contains (according to another legend) the wreck of the first iron ship ever built (by John Wilkinson, whose monument can be seen at Lindale)

Ruin with battlements, Eller How estate.

56

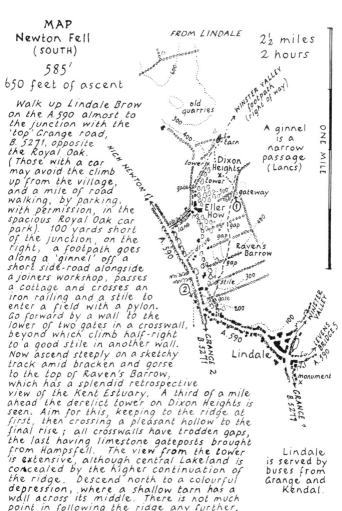

MAP
Newton Fell
(SOUTH)

585'
650 feet of ascent

FROM LINDALE

2½ miles
2 hours

Walk up Lindale Brow on the A.590 almost to the junction with the 'top' Grange road, B.5271, opposite the Royal Oak. (Those with a car may avoid the climb up from the village, and a mile of road walking, by parking, with permission, in the spacious Royal Oak car park). 100 yards short of the junction, on the right, a footpath goes along a 'ginnel' off a short side-road alongside a joiners workshop, passes a cottage and crosses an iron railing and a stile to enter a field with a pylon. Go forward by a wall to the lower of two gates in a crosswall, beyond which climb half-right to a good stile in another wall. Now ascend steeply on a sketchy track amid bracken and gorse to the top of Raven's Barrow, which has a splendid retrospective view of the Kent Estuary. A third of a mile ahead the derelict tower on Dixon Heights is seen. Aim for this, keeping to the ridge at first, then crossing a pleasant hollow to the final rise; all crosswalls have trodden gaps, the last having limestone gateposts brought from Hampsfell. The view from the tower is extensive, although central Lakeland is concealed by the higher continuation of the ridge. Descend north to a colourful depression, where a shallow tarn has a wall across its middle. There is not much point in following the ridge any further, progress being barred by walls beyond a region of disused quarries. Instead, turn left from the tarn by the side of the wall, now on a right of way, descending an improving track past a battlemented ruin (up on the left) to reach a muddy lane at Eller How, where a farm road leads to the A.590. Turn left for the Royal Oak and Lindale.

A ginnel is a narrow passage (Lancs)

ONE MILE

Lindale is served by buses from Grange and Kendal.

57

Hampsfell
727'
700 feet of ascent

from GRANGE-OVER-SANDS
(CLOCK TOWER)

3½ miles
2 hours

Hampsfell is the name commonly used by local people including official bodies, and announced on signposts; Ordnance maps prefer *Hampsfield Fell* (of which 'Hampsfell' is probably a corruption of long standing)

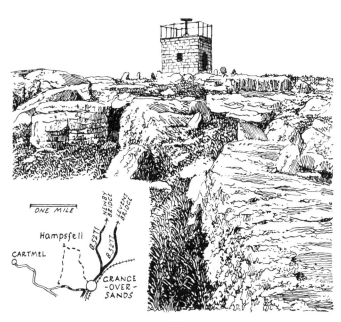

ONE MILE

Hampsfell

CARTMEL

B.5271 NEWBY BRIDGE

B.5277 LEVENS BRIDGE

GRANGE -OVER- SANDS

Grange-over-Sands is blessed with a mild climate, a sheltered and sunny location, fine gardens and lovely woodlands, views across the bay, good shops and an elegant aura of quiet prosperity. It also has Hampsfell.

Hampsfell is a first-rate amenity. It is an elevated ridge of limestone overlooking the Kent Estuary on one side and enjoying a wide prospect of Lakeland on the other. The fell has open access and provides a popular and easy walk with an obvious objective: a stone building known as the Hospice crowning the highest part.

Of Grange's many attractions, Hampsfell is the one most likely to appeal to a semi-retired fellwalker. It is a hill small and unpretentious yet endowed with an air of freedom and space that will recall happy days on greater heights. It is a place for looking northwest, indulging memories, and dreaming.

Limestone pavement on Hampsfell

Lakeland is almost encircled by a narrow belt of carboniferous limestone. Along the northern boundary of the district it is continuous from a point near St. Bees Head to Shap. In the south it is broken, with considerable intrusions in Furness, around Grange-over-Sands and the Kent Estuary, and on the west side of Kendal.

The Hospice, provided by a pastor of Cartmel over a century ago for "the shelter and entertainment of travellers over the fell," is a well-built structure of dressed limestone with an outer flight of steps and a flat roof on which is a view-indicator (added later and unserviceable at the time of writing). The open interior offers good shelter and free poetry readings on painted panels on all four walls: these pronounce as follows, doubtful errors and all —

TAKE NOTICE

ALL PERSONS VISITING THIS "HOSPICE" BY PERMISSION OF THE OWNER, ARE REQUESTED TO RESPECT PRIVATE PROPERTY, AND NOT BY ACTS OF WANTON MISCHIEF AND DESTRUCTION SHOW THAT THEY POSSESS MORE MUSCLE THAN BRAIN. I HAVE NO HOPE THAT THIS REQUEST WILL BE ATTENDED TO, FOR AS SOLOMON SAYS "THOUGH THOU SHOULDEST BRAY A FOOL IN A MORTAR AMONG WHEAT WITH A PESTLE, YET WILL NOT HIS FOOLISHNESS DEPART FROM HIM."

G. REMINGTON

O GOD! O GOOD BEYOND COMPARE!
IF THIS THY MEANER WORKS BE FAIR,
IF THUS THY BEAUTY GILD THE SPAN
OF FADED EARTH AND FALLEN MAN,
HOW GLORIOUS MUST THOSE MANSIONS BE
WHERE THY REDEEMED WELL WITH THEE

THE HOSPICE OF HAMPSFELL

THIS HOSPICE AS AN OPEN DOOR,
ALIKE TO WELCOME RICH AND POOR;
A ROOMY SEAT FOR YOUNG AND OLD,
WHERE THEY MAY SCREEN THEM FROM THE COLD:

THREE WINDOWS THAT COMMAND A VIEW.
TO NORTH, TO WEST AND SOUTHWARD TOO,
A FLIGHT OF STEPS REQUIRETH CARE.
THE ROOF WILL SHOW A PROSPECT RARE.

MOUNTAIN & VALE YOU THENCE SURVEY,
THE WINDING STREAMS AND NOBLE BAY;
THE SUN AT NOON THE SHADOW HIDES,
ALONG THE EAST AND WESTERN SIDES:

A LENGTHENED CHAIN HOLDS GUARD AROUND,
TO KEEP THE CATTLE FROM THE GROUND;
KIND READER FREELY TAKE YOUR PLEASURE,
BUT DO NO MISCHIEF TO MY TREASURE:

THE ANSWER

AND IF THE RICH AND POOR SHOULD MEET
I TRUST THEY WILL EACH OTHER GREET,
AND RICH AND POOR AND YOUNG AND OLD
TOGETHER SCREEN THEM FROM THE COLD:

AND AS THE WINDOWS ARE NOT GLASS'D
WE'LL MIND TO LEAVE THE SHUTTERS FAST,
THE "FLIGHT OF STEPS REQUIRETH CARE"
THEN WHY NOT HAVE A HANDRAIL THERE;
THAT FEEBLE OLD AND TIMID FAIR
MAY MOUNT AND VIEW THE PROSPECT RARE.

THE BLUE AND LOFTY MOUNTAIN'S SIDES
THE NOBLE BAY AND STEALTHY TIDES
THAT TREACH'ROUS CREEP ALONG THE SAND
OR LOUDLY DASH UPON THE STRAND.

YON GAILY RIGGED TRIM PLEASURE BOAT
UPON THE GLITTERING WAVES AFLOAT.
THEN (TURNING TO THE WEST) IS SEEN
DEAR CARTMEL'S PEACEFUL VALLEY GREEN;
MID WAVING WOODS AND VERDENT LANDS,
THE FINE OLD CHURCH OF CARTMEL STANDS.

WITHIN WHOSE WALLS IN DAYS OF YORE
HIS PRIESTLY RULE THE PRIOR BORE.
THEN MAY THE LENGTHENING CHAIN AROUND
KEEP ONLY CATTLE FROM THE GROUND;
FOR NO GOOD MAN WOULD THINK IT PLEASURE
TO CLIMB THE FELL TO SPOIL YOUR TREASURE
YOUR OFFER MADE IN KINDLY SPIRIT
I HOPE YOU'LL FIND OUR CONDUCT MERIT;

CARTMEL 1846

Outside, over the doorway, is an inscription that
will be Greek to most visitors.

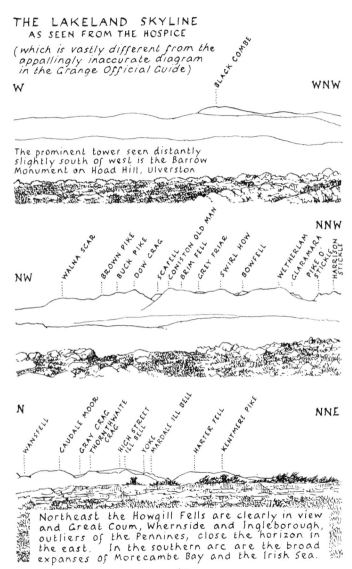

THE LAKELAND SKYLINE

AS SEEN FROM THE HOSPICE

(which is vastly different from the appallingly inaccurate diagram in the Grange Official Guide)

W — BLACK COMBE — WNW

The prominent tower seen distantly slightly south of west is the Barrow Monument on Hoad Hill, Ulverston

NW — WALNA SCAR — BROWN PIKE — BUCK PIKE — DOW CRAG — SCAFELL — CONISTON OLD MAN — BRIM FELL — GREY FRIAR — SWIRL HOW — BOWFELL — WETHERLAM — GLARAMARA — PIKE O' STICKLE — HARRISON STICKLE — NNW

N — WANSFELL — CAUDALE MOOR — GRAY CRAG — THORNTHWAITE CRAG — HIGH STREET ILL BELL — ILL BELL — YOKE — MARDALE ILL BELL — HARTER FELL — KENTMERE PIKE — NNE

Northeast the Howgill Fells are clearly in view and Great Coum, Whernside and Ingleborough, outliers of the Pennines, close the horizon in the east. In the southern arc are the broad expanses of Morecambe Bay and the Irish Sea.

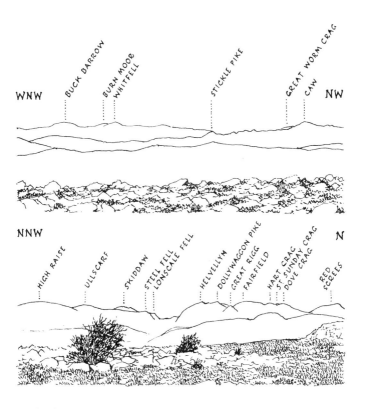

WNW   BUCK BARROW   BURN MOOR   WHITFELL   STICKLE PIKE   GREAT WORM CRAG   CAW   NW

NNW   HIGH RAISE   ULLSCARF   SKIDDAW   STEEL FELL   LONSCALE FELL   HELVELLYN   DOLLYWAGGON PIKE   GREAT RIGG   FAIRFIELD   HART CRAG   ST SUNDAY CRAG   DOVE CRAG   RED SCREES   N

Heights and distances:

BLACK COMBE 1969' 17	SWIRL HOW 2630' 15½	HART CRAG 2698' 19¾
BUCK BARROW 1799' 17	BOWFELL 2960' 19¼	ST SUNDAY CRAG 2756' 21
BURN MOOR 1780' 17½	WETHERLAM 2502' 15¼	DOVE CRAG 2603' 19¼
WHITFELL 1881' 17¼	GLARAMARA 2560' 21½	RED SCREES 2541' 18
STICKLE PIKE 1231' 14½	PIKE O' STICKLE 2323' 19	WANSFELL 1597' 16
GREAT WORM CRAG 1400' 17	HARRISON STICKLE 2403' 18¾	CAUDALE MOOR 2502' 19
CAW 1735' 14	HIGH RAISE 2500' 20	GRAY CRAG 2286' 20
WALNA SCAR 2035' 13½	ULLSCARF 2370' 21¼	THORNTHWAITE CRAG 2569' 19
BROWN PIKE 2237' 13¾	SKIDDAW 3053' 31¾	HIGH STREET 2718' 19¼
BUCK PIKE 2430' 14	STEEL FELL 1811' 20¼	ILL BELL 2476' 17¾
DOW CRAG 2555' 14¼	LONSCALE FELL 2344' 30¼	YOKE 2309' 17
SCAFELL 3162' 20½	HELVELLYN 3118' 22½	MARDALE ILL BELL 2476' 19¼
CONISTON OLD MAN 2635' 14	DOLLYWAGGON PIKE 2810' 21	HARTER FELL 2539' 19
BRIM FELL 2611' 14½	GREAT RIGG 2513' 19¼	KENTMERE PIKE 2397' 18
GREY FRIAR 2536' 15¼	FAIRFIELD 2863' 20¼	

WALNA SCAR · WALNA SCAR PASS · BROWN PIKE · BUCK PIKE · DOW CRAG · GOAT'S HOUSE · CONISTON OLD MAN · BRIM FELL · LEVERS HAUSE · SWIRL HOW · SWIRL HOUSE · BLACK SAILS · WETHERLAM

The beacon on Fell End, looking to the Coniston Fells

From the Clock Tower on Church Hill go past the Post Office and forward up Grange Fell Road, a relentless climb of almost a mile until, beyond the last houses, a path on the right, signposted, crosses a short field by stiles and a farm-lane to enter the rough fell at another stile. A path inclining to the right ascends to an area of boulders and scrub and then proceeds smoothly direct to the Hospice (or a detour can be made to the beacon on Fell End).

Return by a path heading east from the Hospice, passing a large pile of stones like a tumulus where it forks, both branches going down to a cart-track alongside Eggerslack Wood, which, followed to the right, leads to a gate at the top of Hampsfell Road with High Farm nearby but not visited. Hampsfell Road winds pleasantly downhill to the town centre, passing a well-preserved limekiln worth looking at.

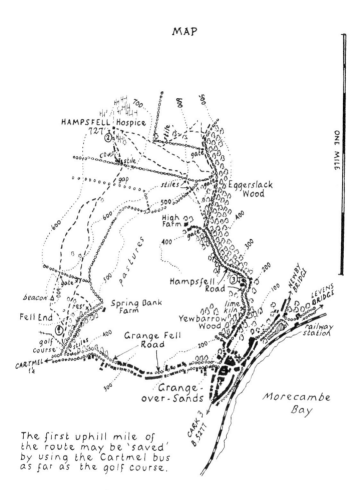

The first uphill mile of the route may be 'saved' by using the Cartmel bus as far as the golf course.

Grange has bus services to Barrow in Furness via Newby Bridge and Kendal via Levens Bridge. Surprisingly in these days of progress, the railway station continues functional, being on the line to West Cumberland and Barrow from Carnforth.

Humphrey Head
172'
200 feet of ascent

Humphrey Head is outside
the National Park boundary

Not by any exercise of the imagination can Humphrey Head be classed as an outlying fell of Lakeland. Outlying it certainly is: a limestone promontory thrusting from the Kent Estuary coast and almost surrounded by mudflats at low tide but awash at high. A fell it is certainly not, being a meagre 172 feet above the sea and, away from its dangerous cliffs, so gentle in gradient and surface texture that the ascent is a barefoot stroll.

ONE MILE

ALLITHWAITE

KENTS BANK

Morecambe Bay

Humphrey Head

Yet its isolation, far-ranging views and seascapes, bird life (of national repute), rocky reefs and interesting approach combine to make the place unique in the district, giving better reason for its inclusion in this book than its omission.

Fellwalkers need an occasional change of scene. Here is one, on Humphrey Head.

The summit

The cliffs of Humphrey Head

Humphrey Head Point

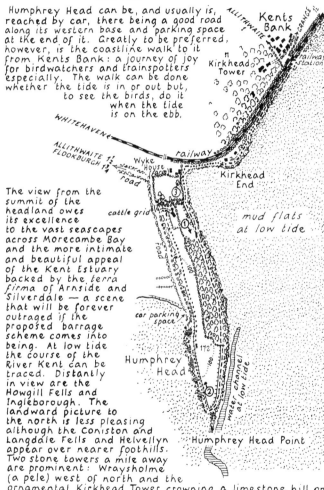

ONE MILE

Humphrey Head can be, and usually is, reached by car, there being a good road along its western base and parking space at the end of it. Greatly to be preferred, however, is the coastline walk to it from Kents Bank: a journey of joy for birdwatchers and trainspotters especially. The walk can be done whether the tide is in or out but, to see the birds, do it when the tide is on the ebb.

Kents Bank

ALLITHWAITE

GRANGE

Kirkhead Tower

railway station

WHITEHAVEN

ALLITHWAITE 1½
FLOOKBURGH 1¾

railway

Wyke House

road

Kirkhead End

The view from the summit of the headland owes its excellence to the vast seascapes across Morecambe Bay and the more intimate and beautiful appeal of the Kent Estuary backed by the *terra firma* of Arnside and Silverdale — a scene that will be forever outraged if the proposed barrage scheme comes into being. At low tide the course of the River Kent can be traced. Distantly in view are the Howgill Fells and Ingleborough. The landward picture to the north is less pleasing although the Coniston and Langdale Fells and Helvellyn appear over nearer foothills. Two stone towers a mile away are prominent: Wraysholme (a pele) west of north and the ornamental Kirkhead Tower crowning a limestone hill on the outskirts of Kents Bank. To the west is the wide flat expanse of Cark Airfield, where parachute jumping (for pleasure!) and other strange pastimes often take place.

cattle grid

road

car parking space

172

Humphrey Head

mud flats at low tide

water channel at low tide

Humphrey Head Point

Cross the rail tracks at Kents Bank Railway Station, using pedestrian gates to get access to the shore. It is common practice to climb over the permanent way boundary wall on the right to reach a concrete parapet on the seaward side of the railway, but if the stationmaster is watching be circumspect and go down a ramp on the left, thence traversing to the right on boulders and so up the sloping seawall to the parapet, which makes an excellent path, single file, alongside the railway for a quarter of a mile. Then, upon reaching some concrete inspection chambers, the railway curves away to the right, the parapet ends and a rough passage over the rocks of Kirkhead End follows: a good vantage point, amongst sea pinks, for observing birds on the mud flats when the tide is out; shelduck, redshank and oyster-catcher being species commonly seen. Around a corner the railway side is again joined and progress over the stones of its embankment is easier to the grassy banks of Wyke House. Here starts Humphrey Head. Go south along the shore, encountering more rocky reefs until a woodland is reached. A path enters the trees and continues closely parallel to the shore: this is a lovely section. When a fence is reached at the end of the wood keep to seaward of it and so arrive at Humphrey Head Point. The fence now turns sharply to climb the easy grass slope to the top of the headland with unprotected cliffs on the left. Go with it, crossing to the Ordnance column (S.5589) on the summit: an excellent viewpoint. Continue forward, descending to a complex of buildings (an Outdoor Centre of the West Riding County Council) and turn left down its access road to join a public road at a cattle grid. Turn right for a few paces, then right again along an old walled lane that debouches on the grassy banks of Wyke House, where the route of the outward journey is rejoined and reversed to the starting point at Kents Bank.

If your wife makes you clean your own boots, as some do, wandering on the mud flats is not recommended.

Bigland Barrow

630'
600 feet of ascent

from NEWBY BRIDGE
4¾ miles
2½ hours

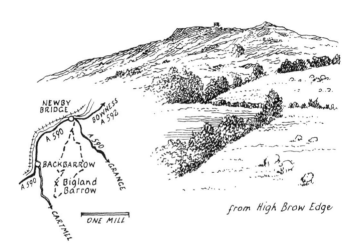

from High Brow Edge

Bigland Barrow rises to the south of the foot of Windermere, not sufficiently to make much impact on the landscape; and it lacks visual appeal in comparison with nearby heights. In spite of its merits as a viewpoint, which are considerable, it is probably most often visited out of curiosity to determine the nature of the unusual manmade adornment on the summit. It lies within a large walled enclosure that, oddly, contains only rough, uncultivated moor (Bigland Allotment), above the 'dolly-blue' village of Backbarrow but is most pleasantly reached from Newby Bridge.

THE VIEW

The views from point 585' and the main top are substantially
the same, but the former is to be preferred because of its
more attractive foreground. The principal Lakeland fells
seen from point 585', looking along the skyline from left to
right, are as follows:

W	the Black Combe range		Fairfield
	Caw	N	Hart Crag
NW	Walna Scar		Dove Crag
	Brown Pike		Red Screes
	Buck Pike		Wansfell
	Dow Crag		Caudale Moor
	Coniston Old Man		Gray Crag
	Brim Fell		Thornthwaite Crag
	Swirl How		High Street
	Bowfell		Froswick
	Wetherlam		Ill Bell
NNW	Pike o' Stickle		Yoke
	Harrison Stickle		Harter Fell
	Pavey Ark	NNE	Kentmere Pike
	High Raise		Shipman Knotts
	Ullscarf		Tarn Crag
	Dollywaggon Pike		Gummer's How

Windermere (lower reaches) is the only lake in view

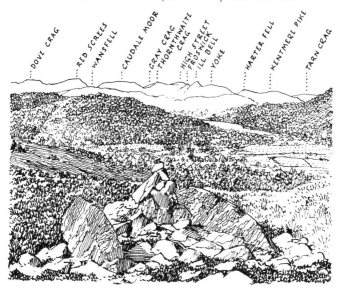

71

From Newby Bridge take the pleasant side-road signposted "Canny Hill" but leave this after 400 yards at a signpost on the right pointing out a path to Backbarrow. A lane, becoming fenced, passes a few residences and reaches a stone wall at a gate and stile. 50 yards further, in open country, follow the left branch at a bifurcation and cross a hollow to rise again gradually to another wall and gate. Beyond, in dense bracken, the path is indistinct. Go forward until abreast of low crags up on the left, when climb steeply to pass them and so reach the Bigland Allotment wall above. Follow this to the right (not easily if the bracken is high) and watch closely for a stile, which use to enter the allotment. Now, first go left to point 585' (the best viewpoint) and then strike south for the main top, Bigland Barrow, which is readily identifiable by its observation tower: a track leads to it from the intervening depression. The top is remarkable not only for its tower – a wartime relic – but also for its willow tree: a reminder that this is really only a very miniature fell. How are the mighty fallen, that we should be nowadays content with such! Remember when we used to trot up Great Gable? However, old age can't be helped (damn it), so descend on a clear path, south, to a gateway in a wall and go round the small tarn ahead to a stile in another wall on the left. This gives access to a pleasant path, which, followed left, winds its way through bracken, heather and gorse, emerging on a leafy farm-road leading to Hazelrigg where it becomes a quiet tarmac lane. Keep to this, bearing left at junctions, and so return to the starting-point at Newby Bridge.

The summit of Bigland Barrow, looking to the Coniston Fells
1: Walna Scar   2: Brown Pike   3: Dow Crag
4: Coniston Old Man   5: Swirl How   6: Wetherlam

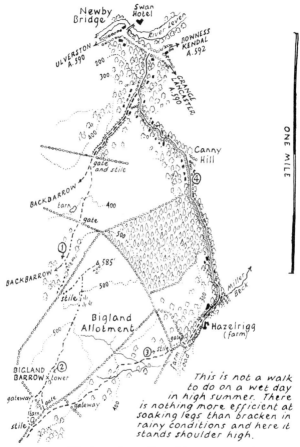

ONE MILE

This is not a walk
to do on a wet day
in high summer. There
is nothing more efficient at
soaking legs than bracken in
rainy conditions and here it
stands shoulder high.

That part of the village of Backbarrow
known as Brow Edge bristles with public footpath signs,
pointing in the direction of Bigland Allotment, without
apparently influencing walkers to follow them. Two
rights of way cross the depression in the Allotment but
cannot be traced on the ground. The only visible paths,
other than sheep tracks, lead to the observation tower.

Finsthwaite Heights

No definite summit.
Highest parts
about 600'.

900 feet of ascent

from NEWBY BRIDGE

5 miles
3½ hours

Throughout this walk the scenery is sylvan with a few pastoral interludes. The only resemblance to fellwalking is in the ups and downs, but in this case the acclivities and declivities occur under foliage.

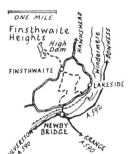

The walk as described is really two short outings combined and the quiet hamlet of Finsthwaite lies midway. The first section is the once-popular climb to the stone tower on the crest of the steep wooded hill at the foot of Windermere; the second part (which can be omitted but ought not to be) is a visit to the lovely Low and High Dams. Everywhere the surroundings are delightful.

But this is not fellwalking.

74

Newby Bridge

Finsthwaite Church

Finsthwaite Tower

This memorial tower-cum-summerhouse is indicated on 2½" Ordnance maps as *Pennington Lodge Tower*. It is no longer kept in repair. A tablet high on the south wall is inscribed as follows:

ERECTED
TO HONOR THE
OFFICERS, SEAMEN AND MARINES
OF THE
ROYAL NAVY
WHOSE MATCHLESS CONDUCT AND
IRRESISTIBLE VALOUR DECISIVELY DEFEATED
THE FLEETS OF FRANCE, SPAIN AND HOLLAND
AND PRESERVED AND PROTECTED
LIBERTY AND COMMERCE
1799

Low Dam

High Dam

Go up the road on the west side of the Swan Hotel (signpost: Lake Side, Sawrey, Hawkshead) and, over the railway bridge, turn left (public footpath sign: Finsthwaite 1) to a pleasant residential backwater where, between two private garages, a woodland path starts a steady climb north.   Ignore an early branch to the left: this is the official right of way to Finsthwaite but is difficult to trace through dense bracken. Instead, keep on forward with a broken wall on the right. A once-popular but now little-used path to Finsthwaite Tower is found on the far side of this wall 200 yards further: cross to it and follow its meanderings steeply uphill amongst mature trees. Take your time; there's no hurry.   A flight of stone steps assists progress at one point; then the path crosses a wall at a broken stile and goes up a bracken slope to meet a more distinct path coming from the opposite direction, the Tower now being seen 40 yards on the right.   It has now no merit as a viewpoint, its former full-length and admirable prospect of Windermere being obscured by foliage.   Return to the nearby junction of paths and continue the walk along the more distinct one, descending gradually and, after two gates, emerging from the wood into open fields. The right of way to Finsthwaite is joined here and followed to the north through three fields, the indistinct path being indicated by stiles and the sight of the church straight ahead.

Finsthwaite has a tuck-shop with an off-licence, and, if the flesh is weak, this is as far as one need go, returning to Newby Bridge by the alternative route shown on the map, to give an all-round trip of 3 miles. Those who are still strong and sober enough to manage an extra 2 miles should leave the hamlet by a private-looking gate almost opposite the shop (public footpath sign: Rusland 2), pass in front of cottages and up a ginnel to a wicket gate and cross a field to a stile in its far top corner, there joining a cart-track curving left up a caravan-bespattered field. Leave the cart-track almost at once and continue on a rising grass path, due north, to a stile and stepping-stones leading into a wood, where the broad path to Low Dam and High Dam is joined and followed. Linger in the delectable surroundings here (it is a much nicer place than the over-populated Tarn Hows) before returning to Finsthwaite by first making a small detour around Low Dam (see map) and then rejoining the path of approach.

Back at the church, take the path signposted 'Lake Side ¾'. It goes through two open fields to enter a fenced woodland lane at a wicket gate and seat.   50 yards in, pass through a gate on the right (the first) and follow a winding path up a pleasant hillside with a lovely view of Windermere behind. The path passes below the Tower (hidden by trees), narrows in a young plantation of spruce, and, after a sharp loop to the left, descends steeply to the Lake Side road, passing a small reservoir rich in water hawthorn.   The road is reached at a rough parking place where some young idiot has carved the word 'ANARCHY' on a tree. He'll learn!   Turn right along the road for Newby Bridge (¾ mile): no sidewalks or verges, so keep out of the way of traffic.

78

MAP

ONE MILE

RUSLAND

High Dam

Low Dam

②

③

Finsthwaite Heights

500

600

400

stile

HAWKSHEAD

stile

300

ROAD

Finsthwaite
+ Church
gate
gate
gate

RUSLAND

gate

LAKE SIDE

300

stile

HAWKSHEAD

400

200

①

500

stile

200

200

Lake Side

gate

400

gate

④

stile

Tower

steps

200

ROAD

stile

200

railway

railway

railway

Swan Hotel

River Leven

RUSLAND

River

BOWNESS
KENDAL
A.592

ULVERSTON
A.590

Newby
Bridge

GRANGE
LANCASTER
A.590

Claife Heights

No definite summit.
Highest parts
   about 900'.

500 feet of ascent

from FAR SAWREY
  5 miles
  3 hours

from Esthwaite Water

Claife Heights is the naturally-wooded and man-afforested upland rising between Esthwaite Water and Windermere. It has not a well-defined summit, the highest point (about 900 feet, north of Pate Crags) having an Ordnance column now lost in conifers and inaccessible, as indeed is most of this upland where Beatrix Potter loved to wander. Its best feature is a series of tarns in lovely settings: reservoirs actually but not obtrusively artificial; none of them appears on 19th century maps. The most attractive of these is Moss Eccles Tarn, which has a glimpse of Windermere and is a charming spot for a siesta. Wise Een Tarn is more open and has a view to the Langdales. Three Dubs Tarn is deeply inurned in a surround of tall trees, and shy: it has a boat-house, better built than most.

Claife Heights is delightful. It was more so before forestry curtailed walking and restricted the views.

Moss Eccles Tarn

Wise Een Tarn

It matters little whether the walk is commenced at Near or Far Sawrey but as the finish is at the latter village it is more convenient to make it the starting point. There is limited roadside parking near the telephone kiosk.

Take the tarmac lane rising on the west side of the Sawrey Hotel, leaving it by a path forking left beyond a cattle grid. Cross a stream (watercress here) and enter a gated lane to join a rough road coming up from Near Sawrey. Follow this to a gate below Moss Eccles Tarn, whence it continues over open ground as a cart-track and, skirting Wise Een Tarn, becomes a less distinct footpath rising into the forest ahead, where it assumes the dimensions of a forest road. At a hairpin bend, a small sign, not very conspicuous, and arrowed H and W (which presumably stand for Hawkshead and Wray) indicates a path going off to the right between the trees (Grass of Parnassus grows alongside it). This is where the fun starts. The way soon becomes distinct underfoot and, in an amazing journey, which in its course zigzags to all points of the compass, enters dense forest. White splashes of paint waymark the path, which is a desperate passage through encroaching and overhanging spruce in many places. At two rocky outcrops, unplanted, there are merciful respites and open views: the first of the Ambleside district and the second, on Pate Crags, of Moss Eccles Tarn and Wise Een Tarn, with Three Dubs Tarn directly below and almost hidden by conifers. Ultimately, just as hope is fading, the old path to Belle Grange from Sawrey is joined at a small signpost and troubles are over, Turn right. The path enters a cart-track and leads back into Far Sawrey (a branch going off to the Windermere Ferry) by the lane coming down on the east side of the hotel.

In 1972 the trees fringing the forest path referred to above were in sad need of pruning. By 1974, failing this attention the path will be impassable. If difficulty and discomfort is experienced, complain to the Forestry Office at Grizedale.

Three Dubs Tarn

(on private ground)

MAP

HAWKSHEAD ← signpost (← H W →)

The path through the forest is arduous. You'll be in a real pickle if you have a coronary here. Try not to.

gap

×viewpoint

Reservoir of the Freshwater Biological Association

800

forest path indicated by white paint

Claife Heights

③

BILLE GRANGE 1

700

Wise Een Tarn

Three Dubs Tarn

signpost

gale

700

viewpoint

Windermere

Moss Eccles Tarn

Pate Crags

800

①

700

600

④

COLTHOUSE

500

400

300

200

gale

private grounds and woodlands

500

600

gale

Righting House

gale

gate HARROW SLACK ½

cattle grid

signpost

gale

NEAR SAWREY ½

500

gate

lane signposted COLTHOUSE AND WRAY

lane signposted HARROW SLACK AND LAKE WINDERMERE

NEAR SAWREY ½ →

400

Far Sawrey

ONE MILE

LAKESIDE

WINDERMERE FERRY 1

83

Latterbarrow

803'

500 feet of ascent

from Hawkshead

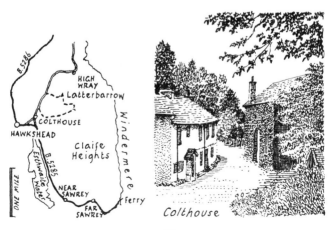

Colthouse

The lily tarn,
Colthouse Heights

Latterbarrow is well known by sight, if not by name, its elegant obelisk being prominently in view from Hawkshead and the Ambleside district. This bare hill, National Trust property, has been spared the forest encroachments from which so much of the west side of Windermere has suffered, and has a deserved reputation as a viewpoint. It is reached by a popular path leaving the Colthouse-Wray road or by a bridleway and a new forest track direct from Colthouse. These two approaches, if linked together, give a circular walk needing little effort yet yielding much delight.

The summit of Latterbarrow,
looking northeast

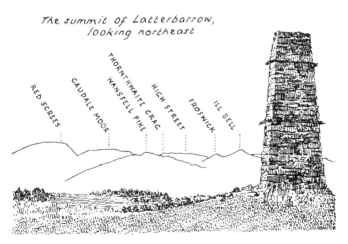

RED SCREES   CAUDALE MOOR   THORNTHWAITE CRAG   MANSFELL PIKE   HIGH STREET   FROSWICK   ILL BELL

The highlight of the walk is the summit of Latterbarrow and it is worth saving until the end. Therefore preferably do the walk anti-clockwise. There is space to park a car (one only) on the roadside near the Latterbarrow gate; if this is used start by walking down the road, south, for a third of a mile to a gate on the left opposite the end of a drive and identifiable by a huge yew near the track leading off. If parked at Colthouse, or coming on foot from Hawkshead, go up the Wray road to this point: it is just beyond Crag Cottage on the right. Miles on the map below are measured from the Latterbarrow gate.

The track past the yew is a public bridleway leading distinctly up the wooded hillside and passing a lily tarn and many noble trees, mainly larch, to arrive at a gate, amongst plantations. Through the gate, at signposts, a stepstile over a high deerfence on the left gives access to a path waymarked by white paint, which, after many changes of direction, leads to an unusual stile near a forestry fire notice. From the deerfence here crossed the path continues up a bracken slope to the monument on the bare top of Latterbarrow. This is a fine viewpoint commanding a panorama of south-east Lakeland, with a mountain skyline ranging from the Coniston Fells to the Ill Bell range above the Brathay and Rothay valleys. Descend by the wide path on the west and so reach the road and the parked car, or go left down to Colthouse.

MAP

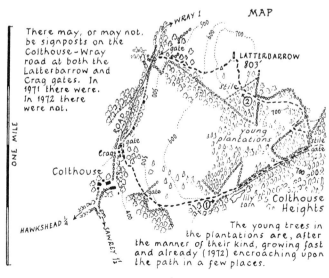

There may, or may not, be signposts on the Colthouse–Wray road at both the Latterbarrow and Crag gates. In 1971 there were. In 1972 there were not.

ONE MILE

WRAY 1

LATTERBARROW 803

gate

stile

②

young plantations

stile gate

Crag

Colthouse

gate

gate

lily tarn

Colthouse Heights

①

HAWKSHEAD ½

SAWREY 1½

The young trees in the plantations are, after the manner of their kind, growing fast and already (1972) encroaching upon the path in a few places.

86

Carron Crag

1025'
750 feet of ascent

3¼ miles
2 hours

HAWKSHEAD

ONE MILE

B 5285

ESTHWAITE WATER

Grizedale Forest

Carron Crag

GRIZEDALE

SATTERTHWAITE

from the
Hawkshead road

Time was when Carron Crag towered prominently above the fifty square miles of undulating country between Coniston Water and Windermere, second only to Top o' Selside in height. This terrain, then open fell and natural woodland, has now become cloaked in the dark shrouds of coniferous forests and Carron Crag has disappeared from view behind a screen of trees. Once it was a landmark, today it is located only by diligent search.

It is doubtful whether anybody ever did in fact look for a needle in a haystack, despite all the publicity given to this practice. If he did, and found it, his elation would be matched by that of a searcher, and finder, of Carron Crag today. Indeed, if the Ordnance Survey maps were not so confident of its existence, its presence in the landscape would not be suspected, so well is it hidden on all sides.

Finding it is more than a triumph of navigation. The Crag itself is a most delightful reward. Here, after the climb through the jungle, one can see the sky again, and feel the sun, and, because the vicinity of the summit is planted thinly, bracken and heather continue to  be rampant around the crest of grey rocks : this is a favourite haunt of the forest deer. A survey column (S.4428) adorns the highest point and still commands a wide prospect — over the treetops.

MAP

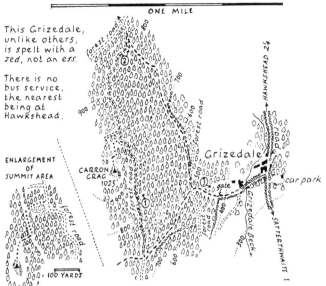

ONE MILE

This Grizedale, unlike others, is spelt with a zed, not an ess.

There is no bus service, the nearest being at Hawkshead.

HAWKSHEAD 2½

800
700
900
600
forest road

Grizedale

ENLARGEMENT OF SUMMIT AREA

CARRON CRAG
1025'

gate
car park

forest road
road
300
400
500
600
700

Grizedale Beck

SATTERTHWAITE 1

100 YARDS

Go down the side-road, past the theatre, over a bridge, and forward to a path signposted 'Coniston Water 3'. Follow this up into the trees: it is stony, even rocky, but distinct. A forest road crosses the route: ignore this and continue ahead, the path now becoming a cart-track, until, after a high wall has come alongside, another forest road is reached. Here turn right on this road for two-thirds of a mile (a kilometre to be strictly correct, but this is a measure of distance we oldtimers will never accept) until, around a sharp bend, an open space on the left, used as a gravel dump (for road making) is reached. Leave the road at this point, cross the open space to a forest ride (fire-break) at its far end, turn left along this and after 100 yards watch carefully for an old track going uphill on the right into the Stygian gloom of trees with a glimpse of daylight ahead. Through this dark tunnel, marking well its place of emergence, the open top of Carron Crag is reached and the Ordnance column soon appears ahead on its perch of rocks.

Return to the forest road and resume the journey along it northwards until a track signposted 'Grizedale' branches off sharply to the right. This returns you to Grizedale, as it says, on a good forest path: a wall joins in on the left (there is an isolated gatepost here that would make you an excellent gravestone) and the way descends pleasantly amid deciduous trees to the first forest road and the path used at the start.

90

fox

pine marten

roe deer

Grizedale Forest

Things have changed in Grizedale. Once it was 'back o' beyond', a secluded retreat thought fit for impounding high-ranking German officers (one got away!). Nowadays the valley presents a lively scene of human activity.

Two developments, interlinked, have caused Grizedale's new look. The Forestry Commission acquired estate land and set to work with a will to transform the fellsides into a great forest, in which they have succeeded well. And then they provided some measure of compensation to the public by opening up the forest and introducing interesting innovations of popular appeal, in which they have also succeeded well. Grizedale Hall, the country mansion that became a prison, has gone: its site is a carpark and lecture place with a warden's office and shop. There are nature trails, forest walks, picnic places, a tree nursery, a wild life museum, a camp site, an information bureau, a high observation tower for the study of birds and animals, even a theatre for celebrity concerts.

badger

Forestry and tourism go arm in arm in Grizedale.

adder

stoat

red deer

Top o' Selside

visiting

a nameless summit, 748'
Low Light Haw, 810'
High Light Haw, 860'
Top o' Selside, 1091'

1050 feet of ascent

from HIGH NIBTHWAITE

4¼ miles

4 hours

from
the nameless summit
at 748'

Between Coniston Water and Windermere lies an undulating expanse of low foothills divided by the Grizedale and Rusland valleys and exceeding a thousand feet in altitude only in a few places.

Much of this upland area has been brought under cultivation in the form of coniferous forests, which now clothe many of the heights to their summits, a development that greatly curtails the freedom of travellers on foot to roam as they will, confining them to a few rights of way and approved nature trails.

But the highest point is as yet inviolate. This is Top o' Selside, overlooking Coniston Water on the east side of the lake and the culminating summit of the rough wilderness of Bethecar Moor. Like many of the smaller fells that carry no frequented paths, the walking is hard although the gradients are gentle, the relatively low altitude, mild maritime climate and unsuitability for grazing inducing a luxuriance in the ground cover — bracken, heather, tough grass — that makes progress even over level ground slow and quite arduous. Top o' Selside and its subsidiary elevations together make an expedition fairly short in distance but demanding in energy. The reward for hard labour is the excellence of the full-length view of Coniston Water and, in other directions, the fine far-ranging prospect of distant horizons.

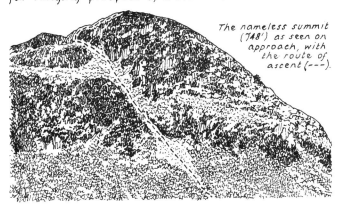

The nameless summit (748') as seen on approach, with the route of ascent (---).

Coniston Water from the 748' summit

1 : WALNA SCAR   2 : BROWN PIKE   3 : BUCK PIKE 4 : DOW CRAG
5 : GOAT'S HAUSE 6 : CONISTON OLD MAN 7 : SWIRL HOW 8 : WETHERLAM
9 : Second cairn at approximately 730'.

Coniston Water from the second cairn

94

THE SUMMIT

The cairn on Top o' Selside remains concealed until the final slopes are breasted and, in the absence of a path on the flat summit plateau, needs to be hunted, the hunt being hampered by deep heather.   The cairn surmounts a little elevation amidst minor undulations and is a pleasant place with a curious sense of isolation due to the disappearance of Coniston Water from view, the prospect around being of wide rolling moorlands and the vast plantations of Grisedale Forest.

HELVELLYN   FAIRFIELD   HART CRAG   DOVE CRAG   RED SCREES

Summit cairn,
Top o' Selside

THE VIEW

The view is very extensive. Although the Coniston Fells hide the central part of Lakeland the panorama is good in all directions, ranging from Black Combe in the west along a mountainous skyline to the Howgill Fells and the Pennines in the east, with Ingleborough prominent. There is a distant view of Blencathra, and, nearer, the Helvellyn and Fairfield ranges fill the northern horizon.

Disappointingly, only the southern tip of Coniston Water can be seen. Arnsbarrow Tarn is the only other expanse of inland water in the picture but seawards there is a wide prospect of Morecambe Bay and its estuaries.

NOTE WELL that the route of ascent described below is suitable only for active and agile walkers. There is an initial very steep and arduous scramble, followed by two miles of wilderness gymnastics in a tangle of bracken and heather: a sore trial to ancient limbs. Its one merit is a classic view of the Coniston Fells across Coniston Water.   Members of Over-60 Clubs, pensioners in general, and others who falter at the prospect of a struggle through virgin vegetation or care not to see the classic view of the Coniston Fells across Coniston Water, are advised to use the return route both ways and enjoy an excellent stroll on a wide path with only a final simple climb to the top.

Leave High Nibthwaite at the barn where the road bends (a telephone kiosk is adjacent and there is space to park a car alongside). Go up the short lane on the north side and through the gate at the end. Turn right on a rising path in bracken above a wall and, around a corner, an abrupt hill appears ahead. This is the nameless point 748' and after crossing a streamlet a track goes off towards it and can be seen climbing up through a patch of scree. Now follows half an hour's unremitting testing of trouser buttons during which time only 200 yards in distance will be gained. The track is excessively steep, loose and slippery; gorse offers prickly handholds. At last a fine cairn rewards toil. But save your camera shots and go on to the next cairn, seen ahead on a sharp rise, crossing a broken wall near a ruin. This is the better viewpoint, the lake being seen perfectly. Now aim east, by the wall, to Low Light Haw, identified by a holly tree, and then leftwards to High Light Haw in direct line with Top o'Selside. Beyond, a small quarry is met in a hollow; then, keeping to the indefinite and undulating ridge (hard going), a path is crossed. Ignore this and continue ahead. When the final slope of Top o'Selside is clearly seen in front, watch for signs of a track leading up it and join this. Now, with its help, faster progress can be made. But when it swings left on a contour plunge forward into deep heather and so reach the summit cairn.

I OUGHT TO HAVE MORE BLOODY SENSE AT MY AGE

Descend due west, crossing the contouring track and continuing down to join a wide cart-track traversing the fellside. Here at last walking becomes enjoyable. Followed to the left this track leads unerringly in two miles to the gate at High Nibthwaite, in lovely surroundings, and affords enchanting views of the lake backed by the Coniston Fells almost all the way.

The ascent of point 748'

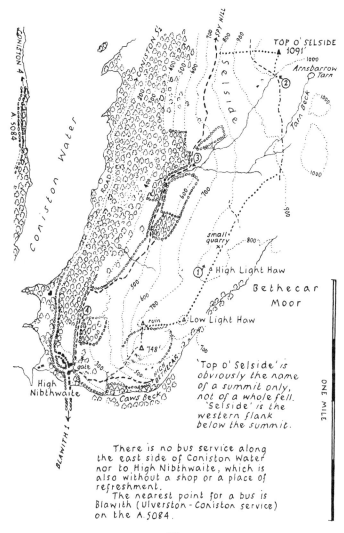

'Top o' Selside' is obviously the name of a summit only, not of a whole fell. 'Selside' is the western flank below the summit.

There is no bus service along the east side of Coniston Water nor to High Nibthwaite, which is also without a shop or a place of refreshment.
The nearest point for a bus is Blawith (Ulverston-Coniston service) on the A.5084.

Beacon Fell
836'

800 feet of ascent

from BROWN HOWE

3½ miles

2 hours

On Ordnance maps the summit is
marked 'Beacon' (part of Blawith Fells)

Beacon Fell ranks amongst the most delectable of
the lesser heights of Lakeland. It is an epitome of
all that appeals to fellwalkers. The approach is a
joy: lovely and colourful terrain rich in trees and
dense thickets of juniper relieved occasionally by
marshy flats of myrtle and dry banks of bracken.
Higher, grey rocks outcrop in haphazard array and
heather and bilberry carpet the rough ground. The
paths are enchanting, full of little surprises, while
the streams are crystal clear. There is a tarn, too,
hidden in a fold of the hills. But it is the summit,
abrupt and rocky, and the far-reaching view that
make the ascent so worth while. One can recline in
comfort here and almost feel sorry for youngsters
who, at this moment, are toiling up Great Gable.

MAP

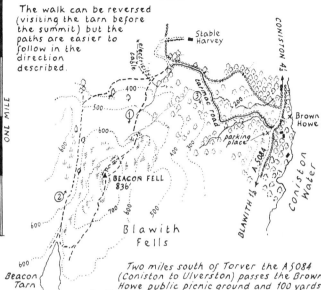

The walk can be reversed (visiting the tarn before the summit) but the paths are easier to follow in the direction described.

ONE MILE

Stable Harvey

CONISTON 4½

Brown Howe

electricity cable

tarmac road

parking place

BEACON FELL 836'

BLAWITH 1½   A5084

Coniston Water

Blawith Fells

Beacon Tarn

Two miles south of Torver the A5084 (Coniston to Ulverston) passes the Brown Howe public picnic ground and 100 yards further a narrow tarmac strip, unsignposted and unenclosed, turns off west at a culverted bridge. There is space for parking just beyond. Cars may be taken along this byroad for ¾ of a mile and there parked, but walking on it is so enjoyable, fringed by a tangle of bog myrtle, juniper, bracken and woodland trees, that it is a pity to hurry over it on wheels. At the upper parking place, on a hairpin bend, a wide green path leads away to the left. Follow this, but just before reaching an overhead cable take a thin track branching up left through the bracken: it soon widens to provide a charming route along an indefinite ridge amongst low outcrops furnished with heather and bilberry. Two streams are crossed, the second in wet ground, the path being obscure here but improving higher, where it climbs a rocky gully (easy, even for us) and then a smaller replica, so reaching the summit cairn, which is defended by low crags: a delightful spot. Continue south along the top to a little promontory where Beacon Tarn comes into view, descending sharply on the right to go down to the head of the tarn by turning right at a prominent rock draped with bell heather. Join a path from the tarn going north over a low col and skirting a marshy hollow (bog myrtle rampant) and a pond (bog bean rampant), then descending through bracken with a pronounced swing to the right to rejoin the outward path at the cable and repeat the walk on tarmac to the A5084.

THE VIEW

The view is restricted by the nearby Coniston Fells, which conceal central Lakeland, but in other directions, especially northeast, is uninterrupted by intermediate heights. The full length of Coniston Water is seen, but of greater interest is the panorama to the south, where Morecambe Bay and the Crake and Duddon estuaries make great indentations of the coastline of the Irish Sea. Industrial smoke rises from the Furness peninsula and the Millom ironworks and the huge quarries of Kirkby Moor appear on the skyline. Far away to the east are the Pennines.

The rocky gully

Principal Fells

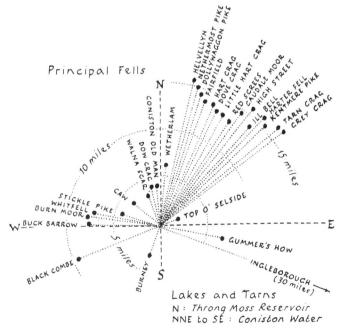

Lakes and Tarns
N : Throng Moss Reservoir
NNE to SE : Coniston Water

WALNA SCAR   BROWN PIKE   BUCK PIKE DOW CRAG   CONISTON OLD MAN   WETHERLAM

The summit of Beacon Fell, looking north to the Coniston Fells

Beacon Tarn

Woodland Fell

visiting
 Yew Bank, 678'
 Wool Knott, 730'

950 feet of ascent

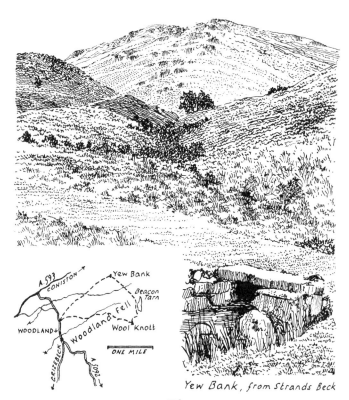

from WOODLAND

5 miles

3½ hours

Yew Bank, from Strands Beck

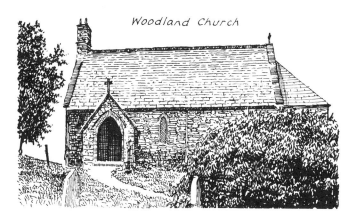

Woodland Church

Woodland Fell is an unfrequented area of heather moors south of Coniston, attracting little attention from walkers whose sights are set on higher targets. It is a region of Lakeland rarely referred to in a fireside study of the map of the district, nor is it a place likely to be recalled in memories.

Yet, on merit, the walk here described is a connoisseur's piece, every step an uninhibited joy, every corner a delight. No footmarks, no litter — this is a miniature wilderness where every explorer treads virgin ground, none too easily when the heather is thick or the bracken high.

Woodland, both valley and fell, is a corner of Lakeland unspoilt by modern development and by-passed by new forms of exploitation. Early man knew the place and left traces of settlements, cairns and walls, while medieval man practiced his primitive industries. But present-day man races past in his car, bound for the Coniston Fells. Perhaps it is asking too much of him to tarry here while yet he is strong and energetic but he would do well to bear Woodland Fell in mind for the time when he is neither. That time will come.

modern cairn
on Yew Bank,
looking to
Beacon Fell

ancient cairn on Yew Bank, looking to Caw

ancient cairn on Tarn Riggs, looking to Wool Knott

The summit of Wool Knott,
looking to Tarn Riggs,
Beacon Tarn and Beacon Fell

The site of the old bloomery,
looking to Bell Knott

There are many traces of medieval bloomeries (hearths
for smelting iron ore) in Lakeland, particularly around
Coniston and Windermere, indicated by heaps of slag
and cinders usually in the vicinity of coppice-woods
and streams. The one illustrated is a fair example:
here the heaps have become thinly grass-covered
except in one place (possibly a recent excavation),
where slag and cinders lie exposed on the surface.

MAP

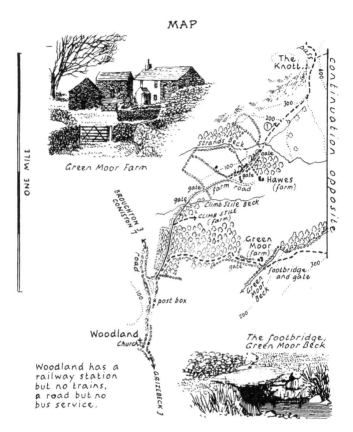

Green Moor Farm

The Knott

continuation opposite

ONE MILE

400

300

200

①

Strands Beck

100

gate
gate
gate

Hawes
(farm)

gate   farm road

gate

Climb Stile Beck

CLIMB STILE
(farm)

Green
Moor
(farm)

gate

footbridge
and gate

Green
Moor
Beck

300

200

BROUGHTON
CONISTON 7
road

100   post box

Woodland
Church

Woodland has a
railway station
but no trains,
a road but no
bus service.

GRIZEBECK 3

The footbridge,
Green Moor Beck

Take your bearings from Woodland Church. The road to
the north forks in 350 yards beyond a postbox (where
the author posted his 1972-3 tax return) and encloses a
triangle of grass: there is carparking space on the link
verge. Then walk along the branch road entering a wood
and keep on the tarmac until, after crossing two pastures
(gates and a placid bull) a wall-corner is reached: here the
road curves to the right to the nearby Hawes Farm but go
forward into a pleasant walled lane (gated) to reach the
open fell at Strands Beck. A lovely path in the bracken, a
joy to tread, now ascends towards Yew Bank, directly in
front: it swings left around the stony slope of The Knott,
rising to a pass overlooking the upper Woodland valley.

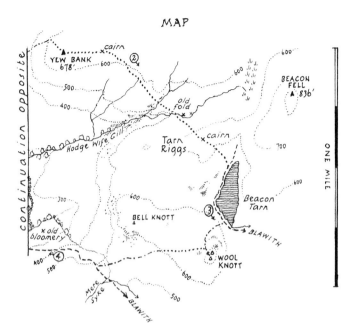

At the summit of the pass follow a thin track climbing up to the right: it fades, but keep on ascending until a view over Coniston opens ahead. To the right now appears the fine cairn on Yew Bank within easy reach. Across the heather, 300 yards due east from the cairn, is a big heap of stones like a tumulus: this, recorded as an old cairn, is visited next. Then aim southeast, crossing two streams in a profound depression and, beyond the second, tackle the steep heather bank facing and so attain Tarn Riggs where there is another ancient cairn. Keep on southeast and descend to Beacon Tarn, following the tarnside path south almost to the outlet, where an indistinct track on the right branches off and curves up to the double top of Wool Knott: a delightful summit. Descend by the same track for 100 yards, then head west down an easy slope, where a path may be found, to join a good bridleway in the depression below. (Give Bell Knott a miss — it is an undistinguished expanse of trackless heather: hard work). The bridleway goes down pleasantly to a slate footbridge at Green Moor Farm: detour en route to the old bloomery if interested. From the farm a charming cart-track runs through woods rich in primroses, anemones, foxgloves and other flora to rejoin the road near the starting point.

Blawith Knott

visiting
Blawith Knott, 806'
Tottlebank Height, 775'

500 feet of ascent

from the
WOODLAND FELL ROAD

2½ miles

1½ hours

The valley of Woodland is wellknown to walkers from the Furness area but hardly at all to others. This quiet backwater lies on the fringe of Lakeland and links the Duddon Estuary with Coniston, once upon a time having a railway.

Woodland is flanked on the east by a continuous line of low fells that look attractive — an impression confirmed by closer acquaintance: this is a region of rough undulations richly cloaked with bracken and heather but patched with rocky outcrops and jewelled by small tarns. Best known of these miniature summits is Beacon Fell, but neighbouring Blawith Knott, a magnificent viewpoint, equally rewards those who climb to its top.

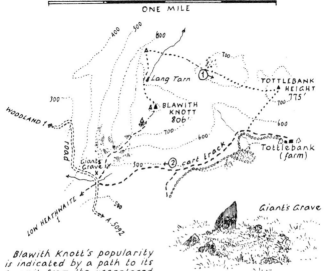

ONE MILE

Lang Tarn

TOTTLEBANK
HEIGHT
775'

BLAWITH
KNOTT
806'

WOODLAND ↑

road

Giants
Grave

Tottlebank
(farm)

cart track

LOW HEATHWAITE ↑

A.5092

Giant's Grave

Blawith Knott's popularity
is indicated by a path to its
summit from the unenclosed
road — a strip of tarmac in
lush bracken — that makes a high-level link between Woodland
and the road summit of the A.5092. 20 yards north of the point
where a cart-track leaves for Tottlebank there is parking space
for a car alongside a culvert conveying a stream under the road.
The path starts directly opposite and skirts outcrops on its way
to the conspicuous cairn, which, upon arrival, is found to be 200
yards short of the highest point, marked by an untidy heap of
stones with a neat cairn nearby.

Most visitors go no further and return the same way, but the
view is too good to be dismissed quickly and is best lingered over
by a leisurely perambulation of the top of the fell.   First head
for the ridge declining in the direction of the Coniston fells; in
the depression between is Lang Tarn, a tiny pool with issuing
stream (a spring, really), which shares with Foxes Tarn, Scafell,
the distinction of being the smallest named tarn in Lakeland.
A cairn along the ridge marks another viewpoint.   From it
aim across the rough but pleasant top, skirting a bouldery
hillock to reach the summit of Tottlebank Height, which has
a glimpse of Coniston Water, and then descend southwest to
join a cart-track and enjoy a simple return along this to the
car with a view of Black Combe directly ahead.

If there is time and energy to spare, consider now an ascent
of the neighbouring Burney (see next chapter). Two peaks in
one day! Quite like old times.....

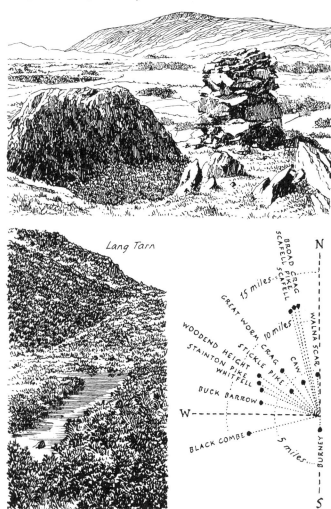

the first cairn, looking to Black Combe

Lang Tarn

N

BROAD CRAG
SCAFELL PIKE
SCAFELL

15 miles

GREAT WORM CRAG

10 miles

STICKLE CRAG
WOODEND HEIGHT
STAINTON PIKE
WHITFELL

CAW

WALNA SCAR

BUCK BARROW

W

BLACK COMBE

5 miles

BURNEY

S

110

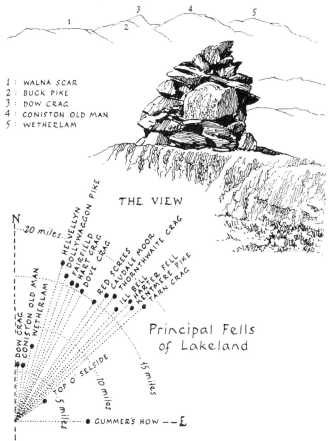

the second cairn, looking to the Coniston Fells

1 : WALNA SCAR
2 : BUCK PIKE
3 : DOW CRAG
4 : CONISTON OLD MAN
5 : WETHERLAM

THE VIEW

Principal Fells
of Lakeland

N — 20 miles

HELVELLYN
DOLLYWAGGON PIKE
FAIRFIELD
HART CRAG
DOVE CRAG
RED SCREES
CAUDALE MOOR
THORNTHWAITE CRAG
ILL BELL
HARTER FELL
KENTMERE PIKE
TARN CRAG

DOW CRAG
CONISTON OLD MAN
WETHERLAM

TOP O' SELSIDE
5 miles
10 miles
15 miles

GUMMER'S HOW — — E

S   On a clear day the view east to south contains
        as much interesting detail as that of Lakeland,
there being an unrestricted prospect of the Howgills,
the fells at the head of Wensleydale, the limestone
group of Great Coum, Whernside and Ingleborough, and
the dark moors of Bowland Forest.   In the southern
sector the lower valley of the Crake and especially
the Duddon Estuary are seen more intimately.

111

Burney
979'
400 feet of ascent

from the
WOODLAND FELL ROAD

1½ miles

1 hour

from Tottlebank Height

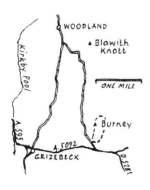

WOODLAND

▲ Blawith Knott

ONE MILE

Burney

Kirkby Pool

A.595

A.5092

GRIZEBECK

B.5281

Burney overlooks the busy main road A.5092 opposite the vast Kirkby Slate Quarries.

On both flanks are scanty remains of antiquities, the rougher west side also having traces of old workings, but in general Burney is featureless, a grassy mound with little to commend it, but redeemed by a superb view that ranges from far out in the Irish Sea to the Yorkshire Pennines and includes most of the southern half of Lakeland.

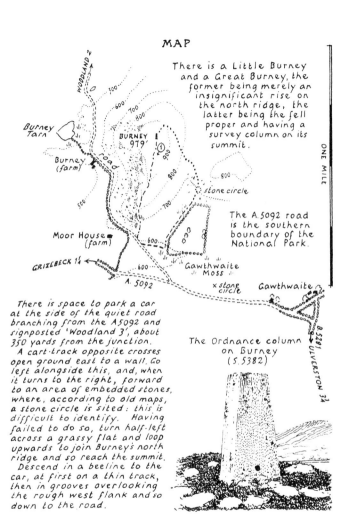

There is a Little Burney and a Great Burney, the former being merely an insignificant rise on the north ridge, the latter being the fell proper and having a survey column on its summit.

WOODLAND 2

BURNEY 979'

Burney Tarn

Burney (farm)

...Road

Moor House (farm)

GRIZEBECK 1¼ ←

A.5092

ONE MILE

stone circle

The A.5092 road is the southern boundary of the National Park.

Gawthwaite Moss

× stone circle

Gawthwaite

B.5281 ULVERSTON 3¼

There is space to park a car at the side of the quiet road branching from the A5092 and signposted 'Woodland 3', about 350 yards from the junction.
A cart-track opposite crosses open ground east to a wall. Go left alongside this, and, when it turns to the right, forward to an area of embedded stones, where, according to old maps, a stone circle is sited: this is difficult to identify. Having failed to do so, turn half-left across a grassy flat and loop upwards to join Burney's north ridge and so reach the summit.
Descend in a beeline to the car, at first on a thin track, then in grooves overlooking the rough west flank and so down to the road.

The Ordnance column on Burney (S.5382)

Considering the modest altitude and ease of access, a most rewarding panorama is revealed from Burney. The view of Lakeland is identical with that detailed in the previous chapter (Blawith Knott) plus the Scoat Fell range. The Duddon estuary is a special feature. East is an uninterrupted 50-mile Pennine skyline.

Walna Scar
2035'
1950 feet of ascent

from CONISTON

8 miles

5 hours

but 2 miles of walking can be avoided by the use of transport to and from Fell Gate

from Red Gill

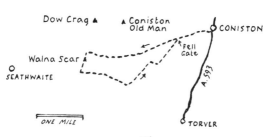

Dow Crag ▲   ▲ Coniston Old Man   ○ CONISTON

Walna Scar

○ SEATHWAITE

Fell Gate

A.593

○ TORVER

ONE MILE

Mention Walna Scar to a Lakeland walker and he will think only of the pass of that name: the route across the fells between Coniston and the Duddon, centuries old, familiar and much trodden. The true Walna Scar, however, is a long grassy ridge elevated only slightly above the summit of the pass and running south of it, forming a section of the eight-mile shoulder of Dow Crag rising out of the Duddon sands. 'Scar' is perhaps a misnomer, there being no rock-faces worthy of mention, but stone is near the surface and a great deal has been gouged from an enormous quarry, now disused, on the west flank. This apart, there is little of interest in the immediate vicinity of the ridge, the greatest motive for its ascent being the superb view it offers, south east and particularly west, in which latter direction there is a wide prospect of the maritime foothills of Lakeland sweeping up to the magnificent grouping of the Scafells.

There are three 'tops', the main one little distant from the pass; the second, of equal height (and an even better viewpoint) is White Maiden, half a mile south; the third, westwards and slightly lower, is White Pike, excelling in its aerial view of Dunnerdale.

The Scafells from Walna Scar

SCAFELL   SCAFELL PIKE   Broad Crag   Ill Crag   GREAT END   ESK PIKE

The Walna Scar Road

The pedestrian route over Walna Scar Pass was originally a road of some importance and known then as Walney Scar Road. Though rough, it followed a course over which horse-drawn vehicles could be taken, and carried much traffic when the many quarries nearby were in use. Today it is no more than a walkers' path, but a very good one, following the line of least resistance between Coniston and the Duddon Valley and providing an easy passage despite its altitude of almost 2000' at the top.   It is no longer the only communication link between the valleys but is still, aesthetically, the best.

MAP

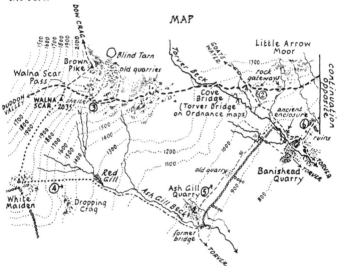

Banishead (known also as Banniside)

The moorland south of the Walna Scar 'road' presents a featureless and dreary scene interrupted only by quarry workings long abandoned, but in fact has yielded many evidences of a Bronze Age settlement.   A stone circle, found to contain two urns and human remains, several cairns thought also to mark burial grounds, an ancient enclosure and a deer trap, make the area of profound antiquarian interest.   The traces, to a layman, are scanty, and not likely to be located without a most diligent search.   How odd that this site of a Bronze Age civilisation should also be the place where a Space-Age flying saucer was first photographed!

116

MAP

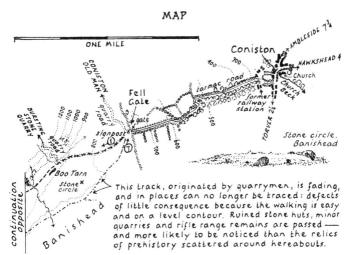

ONE MILE

Coniston

AMBLESIDE 7¾

HAWKSHEAD 4

Church

Church Beck

tarmac road

CONISTON OLD MAN road

400   300

Fell Gate

former railway station

gate

signpost

500

TORVER 2½

CONISTON OLD MAN

1200 1100 1000 900

BURSTING STONE QUARRY

900 800

Boo Tarn

stone × circle

100

200

Stone circle, Banishead

continuation opposite

Banishead

This track, originated by quarrymen, is fading, and in places can no longer be traced: defects of little consequence because the walking is easy and on a level contour. Ruined stone huts, minor quarries and rifle range remains are passed — and more likely to be noticed than the relics of prehistory scattered around hereabouts.

Leave Coniston by the road you used when a lad to go up to the railway station and continue steeply uphill on the tarmac to the intake gate and the open moor — a tiring mile that can be saved by the use of a car. Go forward on the Walna Scar 'road', which has been gravelled for half a mile to serve Bursting Stone Quarry. From Boo Tarn onwards the track reverts to its normal condition. Beyond the two rock 'gateways' the diversion to Goats Water is now very distinct and marked by a large cairn: ignore this and go forward across Cove Bridge on a distinct path to the summit of Walna Scar Pass, which reveals a sudden view ahead to the coastal and western parts of Lakeland. Here turn left up a short and easy grass slope to the cairn on Walna Scar and enjoy a fine panorama. A simple half-mile along the ridge leads to the more rocky top of White Maiden with a wall forming a corner beyond and an aerial view south of the active and internationally-known Broughton Moor Quarry. Now aim east, watching your step amongst initial stones, and descend to the ravine of Red Gill seen below. Turn downstream, a thin path soon forming and leading pleasantly to the buttresses of a collapsed bridge. Cross the stream to the disused Ash Gill Quarry, which has many interesting features to explore. Then take the old quarry track northeast, with a wall on the right, passing through another disused quarry. Cross a path (Torver to Cove Bridge) and continue forward to Torver Beck, fording it to join a wide grass path (Torver to Goat's Water) on the far bank. Turn down this to the right, passing through an ancient enclosure (which will not be noticed) and reaching a huge flooded quarry fed by a high waterfall (which certainly will) — this is a surprising hole, reminiscent of Hull Pot in flood. From its east end strike away across the moor northeast for a mile to rejoin the outward route at the intake gate (known as Fell Gate).

117

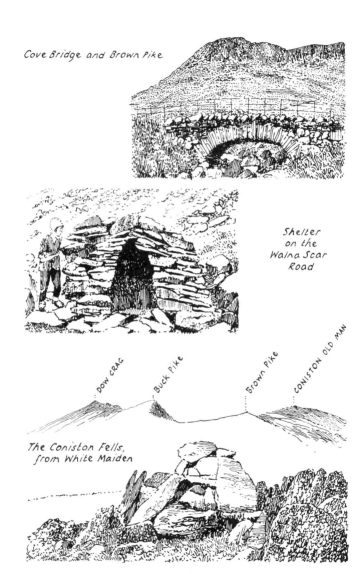

Cove Bridge and Brown Pike

Shelter on the Walna Scar Road

DOW CRAG

BUCK PIKE

BROWN PIKE

CONISTON OLD MAN

The Coniston Fells, from White Maiden

in Ash Gill Quarry

the big hole,
Banishead Quarry

Caw

visiting
Caw, 1735'
Pikes, 1520'
Green Pikes, 1350'

1500 feet of ascent

from SEATHWAITE
(DUDDON VALLEY)
3¾ miles
3½ hours

Caw, from Pikes

Seathwaite

Caw means Calf, but there is nothing docile and gentle in its temperament. In fact, the upper slopes are concave (the Ordnance column can be seen from the valley below) and aggressively steep, being defended by innumerable outcrops of rock, especially to the west, there forming crags. Caw is an abrupt pyramid on the long undulating ridge bounding the lower Duddon Valley on the east with sundry rocky eminences in support. It is a principal feeder of the River Lickle. Slate has been won from a quarry high on the northwest flank and there are minor workings.

Botanically it is rather more rewarding than most fells, yellow saxifrage on the higher slopes and rocks, and bog pimpernel and orchids in the moist pastures below, adding colourful supplements to the commoner flowers, which grow profusely and in great variety.

Summer visitors to the summit may be privileged to see a mating flight of ladybirds. On July 14th.1972 the Ordnance column was alive with them. On the 17th. all had departed.

But it is the view to the Scafells, at any time of year, that will win most hearts. Ladybirds come and go but Scafell is always there. The picture is a classic.

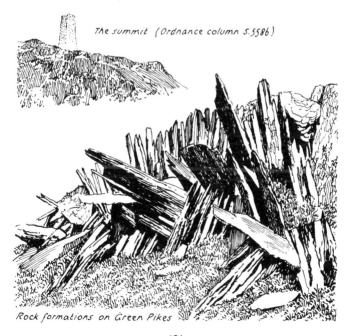

The summit (Ordnance column S.5586)

Rock formations on Green Pikes

ASCENT FROM SEATHWAITE
(DUDDON VALLEY)

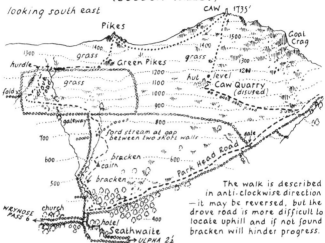

looking south east

CAW 1735'

Pikes

Goat Crag

1300 grass

1400 Green Pikes 1500 grass 1400

hurdle

1300

1200 hut level

grass 1100 Caw Quarry (disused) 1200

fold 1000

900

gateway 800

700 ford stream at gap between two short walls gate

600 bracken 600 Park Head Road

cairn

500 bracken

WRYNOSE PASS 6 church

400

hotel Seathwaite

→ ULPHA 2½

The walk is described in anti-clockwise direction — it may be reversed, but the drove road is more difficult to locate uphill and if not found bracken will hinder progress.

There is parking space in front of the Newfield Hotel at Seathwaite, but get permission (in case the brewery wagon is due). Start along the road by the side of the hotel, going towards the church, but leave it at the first bend and keep ahead into a rough lane with three gates (used for penning sheep), then turning right on a cart-track, stony in places, alongside a wall running diagonally across the fell. This is 'Park Head Road', formerly of some importance when the quarries were working, as the bridged streams testify, but now merely a pleasant and little-used footpath: watch for ants if you sit down. After a mile, beyond a gate, a branch turns sharply left and leads to Caw Quarry: this is the way to go. (Park Head Road continues over a pass en route for Broughton Mills, but abandon any idea of using it further to climb Caw by its west ridge, which is both steep and very craggy). The quarry road, supported by a retaining parapet, is easy to follow to its end, where there is shelter, if need be, in a stone hut. Then climb past an old level and straight up the fellside: it is fairly steep and without a path but quite easy. If your navigation is as good as it used to be you will duly arrive at the Ordnance column on the rock ridge forming the summit.

Old level, Caw Quarry

continued

MAP

continued

Descend from the summit by the eastern slope, keeping left at first to avoid outcrops, and cross a depression to scramble up amongst handsome rocks to the cairn on Pikes, where turn north to reach the intake wall over the top of Green Pikes.   Follow the wall to the right to the only opening in it: a gateway with a hurdle. Over this, a drove road goes down the fellside in twists and loops to Seathwaite: its beginnings are obscure but it is revealed as a grassy groove lower down.   Watch the map to check its meanderings where its direction is not clear on the ground; with luck it can be followed all the way, and when the bracken is high it is worth searching. It is indefinite in the final pasture, where aim for the 3-gated lane.   The brewery wagon might have been when you get back to the hotel. Cheers!

The view is one of depth as well as distance, the abrupt summit being sufficiently elevated above its supporting slopes to give an uninterrupted downhill view into the deep enclosing valleys of the Duddon and the Lickle. Especially good is the full-length prospect of Upper Duddon, looking from Seathwaite in a bower of trees to the lofty rim of mountains around the head of the valley, and, over Hard Knott, those enclosing Eskdale: a lovely scene of tranquillity harmoniously blending with sterility. The nearer Coniston Fells are not so favourably displayed, only the featureless western slopes being seen. Far away in the east is the skyline of the Pennines, with Ingleborough dominant. Southwards one surveys Morecambe Bay as from an aeroplane, with the estuary of the Duddon in intimate detail. The position of Ulverston is indicated by the Barrow Monument on Hoad Hill and that of Seascale by the towers of the Atomic Power Station, which has the knack of despoiling every view in which it appears.

Principal Fells

Lakes and Tarns

SW: Stickle Tarn
WNW: Devoke Water
NNE: Seathwaite Tarn
ESE: Coniston Water
    (two sections)
SE: Beacon Tarn

THE VIEW

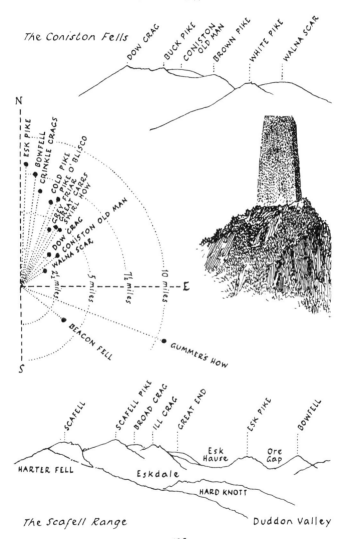

The Coniston Fells

DOW CRAG
BUCK PIKE
CONISTON OLD MAN
BROWN PIKE
WHITE PIKE
WALNA SCAR

N

ESK PIKE
BOWFELL
CRINKLE CRAGS
COLD PIKE
PIKE O' BLISCO
GREAT CARRS
GREY FRIAR
SWIRL HOW
DOW CRAG
CONISTON OLD MAN
WALNA SCAR

2½ miles
5 miles
7½ miles
10 miles

E

BEACON FELL
GUMMER'S HOW

S

SCAFELL
SCAFELL PIKE
BROAD CRAG
ILL CRAG
GREAT END
Esk Hause
ESK PIKE
Ore Gap
BOWFELL

HARTER FELL
Eskdale
HARD KNOTT

The Scafell Range
Duddon Valley

125

Stickle Pike

visiting
Great Stickle, 990'
Tarn Hill, 1020'
Stickle Pike, 1231'
a nameless summit, 1183'
The Knott, 925'

1700 feet of ascent

from BROUGHTON MILLS

5¼ miles

5 hours

This walk may be
described as
"The Dunnerdale
Horseshoe"
(bearing in mind
the note below)

from the south

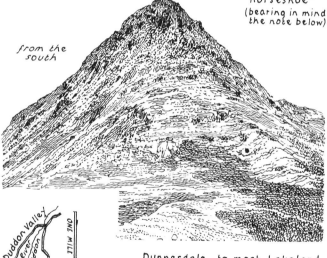

Dunnerdale, to most Lakeland visitors, is the valley of the River Duddon, this being the name of the parish, but the true Dunnerdale is, geographically, a side-valley of the River Lickle two miles in length and watered by Dunnerdale Beck, quite independent of the Duddon. Nor should Stickle Pike and Stickle Tarn, referred to in this chapter, be confused with places of like name in Langdale — they are a day's march away.

The Dunnerdale Fells are low in stature, small in extent and insignificant on the map, yet they assert themselves on the local landscape in a bristly defiance of accepted mountain standards. Of course they are not worthy of comparison with Scafell or Great Gable, but they refuse to admit it. Where else in Lakeland is there so rugged a skyline? Where else, outside Skye, is there an array of peaks so crowded? Well, there is something in their claim. Here, certainly, is an upland tormented by a confusion of crags and peaked outcrops: all in miniature, amounting to nothing, really, in the general lie of the land, but with a magnetism that compels the eye and challenges the feet. Picnic parties by the lower Duddon notice the pugnacious, rather impudent beginning of the group in the sharp rocky turrets rising out of steep bracken slopes; walkers in the valley of the Lickle see their eastern aspect as a serrated skyline of abrupt upsurges and downfalls, a chaotic jumble of mini-summits.

The kingpin of this area is Stickle Pike, a mere 1231 feet above the sea yet a budding Matterhorn with many juvenile satellites.... But it is all make-believe, really, all pretence. To do the round of the ridges is actually quite simple. The aggressive appearance from below is belied on acquaintance ..... there are no dragons on these tops, no menace in their rocks. Instead there are lovely tarns where asphodel and cotton grass and bogbean colour the shallow waters, adding gaiety to the scene and scenting the air, lichened boulders bright with parsley fern, soft carpets of turf and bracken, innumerable pleasant couches where one can lie in comfort and think of real fells like Scafell and Great Gable. But do not voice these thoughts: Stickle Pike is proud and easily hurt.

Stickle Pike
from
Great Stickle

Some walks have obvious beginnings and follow so natural a line that directions are not really necessary. This one is not in that category. It is not easy to see, at Broughton Mills, how to get a footing on either of the two ridges that rise from the maze of woodlands and walled fields above the hamlet, nor at this distance to identify precisely the fells peeping over the trees. Only the Knott is clearly in view.

However, the thing to do is to get started correctly, and, over the bridge across the Lickle, a tarmac lane with a signpost 'Ulpha. Not for motors' points the way to go. The tarmac ends at the first farm, Green Bank, and there is no further guidance by signs, here or beyond. Without entering the farmyard, take a rough lane uphill as far as a cottage, opposite which a thin and stony track winds up into a wood with a wall on the left. The signpost was right: this is not a way for motors. Escape at a gate from the clutches of foliage and continue ahead, turning sharp left after 80 yards into a lane, which contours the slope, rising and falling slightly, and reaches the open fell at the last of three gates, above a barn. The shapely Hovel Knott appears ahead: contour around its base, still on a path, and ascend its far slope of bracken, where walls are left behind and a col crossed. Little Stickle is now close on the right. The main path here starts to descend to Ulpha: take a less distinct branch forking right and follow it up to the ridge, where a detour to the right leads to the Ordnance column (S.5453) on the abrupt summit of Great Stickle. The main objective, Stickle Pike, is now in view to the north. Reach it by a beeline or preferably by keeping to the indefinite ridge over the well-named Tarn Hill to the depression below the sharp rise to the Pike. (Note a small circle of stones on a patch of grass in this depression: it marks the site of an ancient cairn). Don't tackle Stickle Pike directly up its steep front but find and follow a thin path that ascends gently to a col on its east side, arriving at a cairn from which a line of footmarks climbs steeply left to the summit: a fine vantage point. Having got your wind back, go down to the cairn on the col, joining a wide grass path that passes near to Stickle Tarn on its gentle descent to the top of the road now in sight ahead. (This path is obviously the tourist route to the Pike from cars parked on the verge). The road links Broughton Mills and the Duddon Valley, and provides a quick way back to the starting point (right not left) if your legs are buckling. Those who are damned if they'll give in should cross the tarmac to a path going forward to the extensive Stainton Ground Quarries and ascend amongst the spoil heaps to the topmost hole. A slanting course half-right now climbs easily to the second of the walks two ridges (and the least interesting). Go along this to the right, over point 1183' but skirting Raven's Crag to the left and descend to a depression beyond which is a simple walk to the big cairn on the Knott. Take a last look round (most of the route is visible from here), then descend due south, keeping to grass rather than bracken, and, with the farm of Knott End well to your right, reach a gate at the foot of the slope giving access to a tarmac road, which follow downhill, joining the valley road, passing the church and so returning to Broughton Mills pleased with yourself. A very good performance, considering your age.

MAP

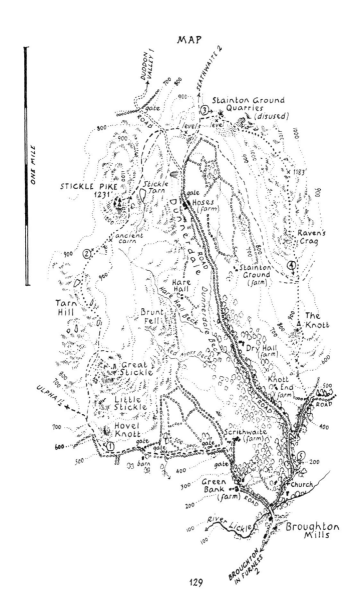

DUDDON VALLEY 1

SEATHWAITE 2

700

800

900

gate

ROAD

③ Stainton Ground
Quarries
(disused)

level · level

800

900

1000

STICKLE PIKE
1231

Stickle
Tarn

× 1183'

900

800

Dunnerdale
ROAD

gate

Hoses
(farm)

900

800

Raven's
Crag

ancient cairn

② 900

900

Tarn
Hill

Hare
Hall

Hare Hall Beck

Dunnerdale Beck

Dunnerdale ROAD

Stainton
Ground
(farm)

④

Brunt
Fell

Red Moss Beck

The
Knott

800

900

Great
Stickle

Dry Hall
(farm)

ULPHA 2

700

800

Little
Stickle

Knott
End
farm

ROAD

500

Hovel
Knott

500

①

gate

gate

barn

500

600

700

Scrithwaite
(farm)

gate

ROAD

400

500

⑤

200

400

gate

400

Church

300

Green
Bank
(farm)

ROAD

200

200

River Lickle

100

100

Broughton
Mills

BROUGHTON
IN FURNESS 2

ONE MILE

Stickle Pike

Mountain summits are especially attractive when they are rocky, abrupt on all sides, small in extent and exciting. These are attributes in which Stickle Pike's top scores over those of many a higher and better-known fell. It has also the added appeal of a shapely cairn on a natural plinth: a rock outcrop on the highest point.

A second cairn occupies the south end of the short and undulating ridge forming the summit; other baby ones are sprouting as a result of the playful activities of its Sunday afternoon visitors from cars on the nearby road.

The view is good within the limitations imposed by the modest altitude. The high skyline of the Pillar, Scafell, Bowfell and Coniston groups forms an effective horizon to the north but much of the detail of these mountains is obstructed by the nearer Harter Fell and Caw, which stand like sentinels above the lovely Duddon Valley. In other directions the scenes are mainly coastal with the estuary and lower reaches of the Duddon, backed by a full-length Black Combe range, intimately prominent.

Near the beginning
of the walk —
        Hovel Knott

Near the end of the walk —
        Cairn on The Knott,
        looking to Raven's Crag and Caw

Dunnerdale Fells

920'

from STONESTAR

800 feet of ascent

2½ miles

2 hours

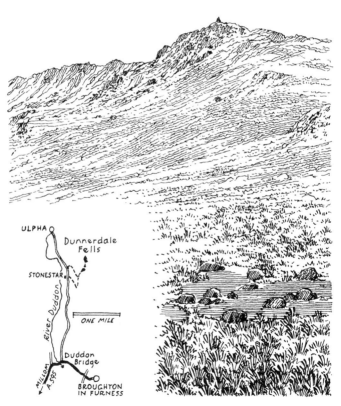

The lower part of the Duddon Valley is no less beautiful than the higher reaches, even though the enclosing fells are of miniature proportions in comparison; and, in particular, the eastern ridge between Ulpha and Duddon Bridge, across the breast of which runs the motor road, is of special eye-catching appeal. A fringe of crags and scree forms a ragged but attractive skyline defended by steep slopes of dense bracken and scattered tors of naked rock. The highest point on the skyline, when viewed from the road, is crowned by a cairn, and this summit, which has the merit of looking loftier than it actually is is the objective of the walk described. It must be stated, however, that the traverse of the fell, once the ridge is attained, does not provide the excitement promised from below, the feature of most interest being a remarkable profusion of ancient cairns. When the summit is reached it is found to be overtopped by the fells described in the previous chapter, a small depression with a few tarns separating it from Tarn Hill.

The knoll on which the cairn stands has not a distinctive name. The Ordnance Survey adopt the general name of Dunnerdale Fells for this upland area east of the lower Duddon.

The path up from
Stonestar

The fellside rises above the road gradually at first and then quite steeply to the summit ridge; but, at one point, on the top of a stony bluff, there occurs a natural level terrace, now a bracken meadow. This flat area is bounded by a low parapet, obviously the footing for a wall that has been scattered or buried in moss and vegetation over many centuries. The plan of the enclosure, despite obscuring bracken, is still plain to see when the site is visited but not apparent from a distance, and not easy to locate. A tumbled  wall along the top of the bluff and on the line of the original wall appears more recent and probably served to stop sheep from straying onto steep ground. To the south, across a beck with a sheepfold and on the same contour, are fragmentary remains of other old walls.

Earlier Ordnance maps recorded the site as 'Stone Walls', using old-style lettering to indicate antiquity. Enough remains, with the many ancient cairns in the vicinity, to confirm the existence of a former settlement in this area.

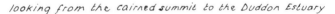

looking from the cairned summit to the Duddon Estuary

MAP

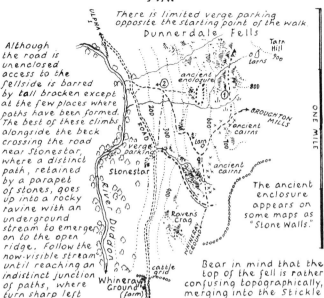

There is limited verge parking
opposite the starting point of the walk.

Dunnerdale Fells

Although
the road is
unenclosed
access to the
fellside is barred
by tall bracken except
at the few places where
paths have been formed.
The best of these climbs
alongside the beck
crossing the road
near Stonestar,
where a distinct
path, retained
by a parapet
of stones, goes
up into a rocky
ravine with an
underground
stream to emerge
on to the open
ridge. Follow the
now-visible stream
until reaching an
indistinct junction
of paths, where
turn sharp left
and contour level
ground where ancient
cairns occur in profusion
and can be counted by
the dozen. After crossing
a beck as it enters a ravine

The ancient
enclosure
appears on
some maps as
"Stone Walls."

Bear in mind that the
top of the fell is rather
confusing topographically,
merging into the Stickle
Pike complex. The ridge,
too, is indefinite. Nor do
the visible paths accord in
all respect with those on
the Ordnance Survey maps.

and passing a prominent holly a good track is joined and
followed to the right, rising past a bouldery tarn. Now keep
an eye on the cairned summit directly ahead (our objective)
for the path veers right and reveals the more prominent and
bulkier Great Stickle and Tarn Hill quite near (but not on our
programme today). Make a beeline for the cairned summit
by leaving the path to cross a marshy depression and tackle
the bracken slope beyond: hard going, but the cairn is near
and soon reached by a determined effort. The cairn stands on
a grassy knoll, with a smaller one surmounting a higher point
30 yards further.
The top is fringed by tiers of crags and thick bracken on the
Duddon side and although a direct descent is practicable by
way of the ancient enclosure it is better to return along the
route of ascent as far as the holly tree, where continue on
the good path across the fellside and down to the road, up
which a quarter-mile walk returns you to the car. Or try to
locate a bracken-choked path that leads straight back from
the 300' contour to the starting point and avoids road-walking.

Great Worm Crag

1400'

750 feet of ascent

from the
BIRKER FELL ROAD

3½ miles

2½ hours

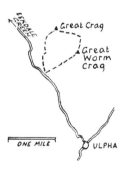

Great Worm Crag is typical
of the many lesser fells that
walkers in the early flush of
enthusiasm do not trouble to
visit while greater heights
remain unscaled, and even
later the old favourites are
often still first choice for a
day on the tops. Some walkers
have climbed Great Gable a
hundred times but never set
foot on Great Worm Crag. Yet
this humble and **neglected** fell
offers a rewarding service to
those whose active days on the
hills are nearly over, for here
is an excellent belvedere for
viewing again intimately the
mountains of yesteryear.

Ancient cairn, Great Worm Crag

The approach to
Great Crag

Great Crag

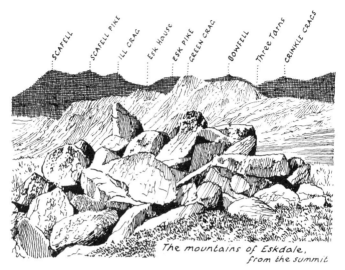

SCAFELL · SCAFELL PIKE · ILL CRAG · ESK HOUSE · ESK PIKE · GREEN CRAG · BOWFELL · Three Tarns · CRINKLE CRAGS

The mountains of Eskdale,
from the summit

Great Worm Crag is a simple but tedious climb when done directly from the road along its base. Interest is added in the form of rock scenery if the roundabout way mapped opposite is taken.

Approaching from Ulpha by the Eskdale fell road, a car may be parked in a recess on the left 180 yards short of the Woodend junction. The old path across Birker Fell is now indistinct and its point of departure from the road obscure, but the start is marked by a flat stone in the ditch 100 yards back along the road. The path, a thin trod, aims north over the moor on the same contour, left of Great Worm Crag, and skirts Sike Moss: two cairns on boulders are a help. Highford Beck is crossed after a mile and the line of crags ahead to the right then tackled. No trouble is encountered on Little Crag. Beyond is Great Crag, a big rock mass with impressive cliffs: this can be skirted along its base, or, if you are feeling a bit of a devil, it can be traversed after a stiff initial scramble. Now in view are the more formidable ramparts of Crook Crag and Green Crag, a mile distant, but happily this rough area was dealt with in 'The Southern Fells' and needn't concern us today. Instead, aim for the headwaters of Highford Beck, taking White Crag in your stride, then head south up an easy slope to the two cairns on Great Worm Crag. A mile-long beeline down to the road and the car, over easy terrain, ends the walk. The Ordnance map indicates many ancient cairns on this final slope, but only one specimen, a good one, is likely to be seen on the descent.

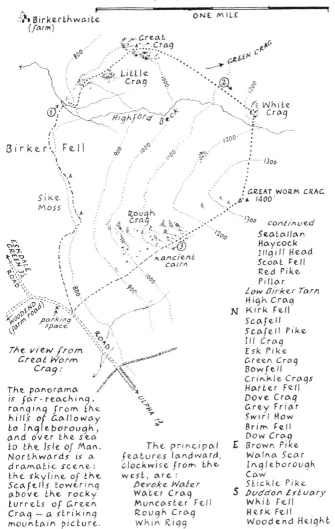

ONE MILE

Birkerthwaite (farm)

Great Crag

Little Crag

GREEN CRAG

White Crag

Highford Beck

Birker Fell

Sike Moss

Rough Crag

ancient cairn

ESKDALE GREEN ROAD

WOODEND (farm road)

parking space

ROAD

ULPHA 1¼

GREAT WORM CRAG 1400

1300

1200

1100

1000

900

800

The view from Great Worm Crag:

The panorama is far-reaching, ranging from the hills of Galloway to Ingleborough, and over the sea to the Isle of Man. Northwards is a dramatic scene: the skyline of the Scafells towering above the rocky turrets of Green Crag — a striking mountain picture.

The principal features landward, clockwise from the west, are:

Devoke Water
Water Crag
Muncaster Fell
Rough Crag
Whin Rigg

continued
Seatallan
Haycock
Illgill Head
Scoat Fell
Red Pike
Pillar
Low Birker Tarn
High Crag
N Kirk Fell
Scafell
Scafell Pike
Ill Crag
Esk Pike
Green Crag
Bowfell
Crinkle Crags
Harter Fell
Dove Crag
Grey Friar
Swirl How
Brim Fell
Dow Crag
E Brown Pike
Walna Scar
Ingleborough
Caw
Stickle Pike
S *Duddon Estuary*
Whit Fell
Hesk Fell
Woodend Height

Hesk Fell

visiting
Hesk Fell, 1566'
The Pike, 1214'

1100 feet of ascent

from the
BIRKER FELL ROAD

4¾ miles

3 hours

Hesk Fell,
from
The Pike

Hesk Fell has many shortcomings but at least has the one merit of honesty. Its appearance promises nothing at all of interest and the trudge to its featureless summit confirms first impressions. It is a massive grassy mound between the Duddon and Esk valleys, and dominates the Birker Fell road. A good view of the Scafell group is the only reward for its ascent. It is rarely climbed. A dependency, The Pike, has a certain charm of surroundings the parent fell lacks and has much the better summit.

140

right:
Ulpha Church

below:
The mountain skyline at the head of Eskdale as seen from Hesk Fell

SCAFELL   SCAFELL PIKE   ILL CRAG   Esk Hause   ESK PIKE   BOWFELL

The detour to The Pike

An old enclosure
Hesk Fell

141

Before starting this description of the walk, it must be mentioned again that Hesk Fell is a very dull climb. It looks uninteresting, and it is. Nobody will ever drop dead with excitement or suffer spasms of emotion on an ascent of Hesk Fell.

Approaching from Ulpha by the Eskdale fell road, a car may be parked in a recess on the left 180 yards short of the Woodend junction. Start the walk by going along the Woodend road until, at a gate with a prominent tree, it turns away amongst walled fields. Here continue forward up the open fell alongside the intake wall until this also turns away. From this point the summit of Hesk Fell is on a compass bearing due south, but progress is rather easier by looping round to the skyline of the rising ridge.   The ground is everywhere spongy and featureless and the only interest during the simple and tedious climb is found in the retrospective view of the Eskdale mountains, which improves with every step Pulses quicken when a solitary stake is seen, but it signifies nothing. Further, the flat top, innocent of any sign that it has been visited before, is reached, the highest point being a matter of personal decision. The panorama of the Pillar, Scafell and Coniston groups is excellent, but, having surveyed it, with a wish that you were there instead of here, the unattractive top offers no other inducements to linger. Descend southeast in the direction of The Pike. On this flank the ground is drier and more pleasant underfoot.   Surprisingly, the fellside here is littered with clusters of old walls forming small enclosures : one can remember no reference to these nor are they indicated on Ordnance maps, the conclusion being that they are merely small bields or sheep-shelters and not the remains of a primitive settlement Aim for the gate in the wall ahead. The detour to The Pike starts and returns here and may be omitted. If the hour it takes can be spared and the legs are willing, surmount the gate and follow the wall, first downhill and then up, pointing like an arrow to the summit. The Pike is delightful (compared with Hesk Fell). The cairn, over the wall, stands on the edge of a profound declivity with the woods and fields and toy cottages of the Duddon Valley charmingly displayed below: after seeing this superb aerial view, even Hesk Fell may be forgiven.

Return to the gate and contour the open slopes above the intake wall, to the right. Sheep tracks are a help. The eye of imagination, still influenced by the possibility that this fellside may have a history hitherto unsuspected, pictures many stone circles amongst the scattered boulders, but the existence of a large enclosure with now-crumbled walls is undeniable. Crosby Gill, in wet surroundings, must now be crossed to get back to the car: tread the marshy ground gingerly. The stream may be negotiated at several points, but not without hazard. The 'official' stepping-stones are half-submerged. Safely across, a prominent cairn-mound (this at least is of undisputed antiquity) is passed on the way back to the road. Note that if Crosby Gill is in spate, a dry-shod crossing can be made via the Woodend road bridge.

142

MAP

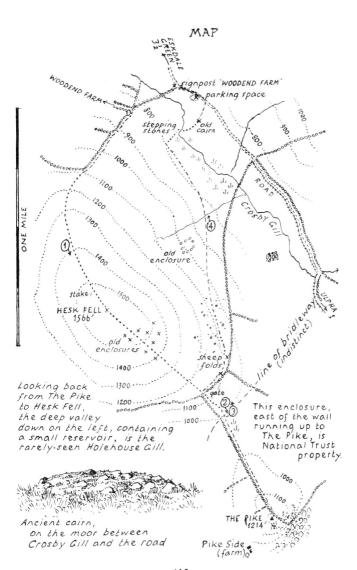

The Circuit of Devoke Water

visiting
Rough Crag, 1049'
Water Crag, 997'
White Pike, 1370'
Yoadcastle, 1610'
Woodend Height, 1597'
Seat How, 1020'

1450 feet of ascent

from the
ULPHA-ESKDALE
FELL ROAD

5½ miles

4 hours

ESKDALE GREEN

ONE MILE

Rough Crag
Water Crag
Seat How
Devoke Water
White Pike
Woodend Height
Yoadcastle

Birker Fell

ULPHA

The cairn on White Pike

Woodend Height (left) and Yoadcastle, from White Pike

The large tarn of Devoke Water, a popular resort of anglers and bathers, occupies a shallow basin in a surround of low fells, the tops of which yield the finest of all views of the mountains circling the heads of Wasdale, Eskdale and the Duddon Valley: an exciting background seen in sufficient detail to engage the attention throughout the tour here described, which is a circuit of all the heights overlooking the tarn. The views westward of the Esk estuary and the coastal plain beyond are also excellent, although sadly marred by the presence of the atomic power station, and a wide seascape includes the Isle of Man. The summits visited are varied in character with rocky bluffs outcropping in many places, and on the north side of the tarn granite boulders attractively adorn heather slopes and ancient cairns add an antiquarian interest— but it is predominantly for the mountain prospect that this walk gains a strong recommendation.

Yoadcastle, with Whit Fell behind, from Woodend Height

The summit of Rough Crag

The summit of Water Crag

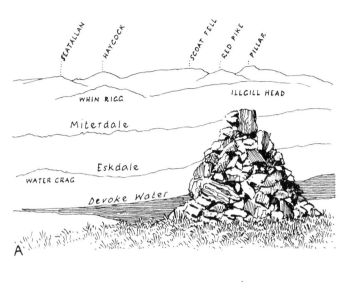

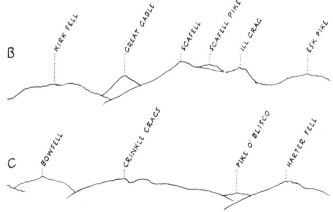

Views from Woodend Height:
A: *looking north*: the Pillar group
B: *looking north-north-east*: the Scafell group
C: *looking north-east*: the Bowfell group

The fell road between Ulpha and Eskdale, unenclosed for much of its distance and affording beautiful views, arrives at a signposted crossroads where a wide track (indicated as a bridleway to Waberthwaite) turns off to Devoke Water: nearby is verge-parking for cars. Follow this track (on foot) until, beyond a gate, Devoke Water comes into view ahead, then aim over a heather slope on the right to Rough Crag: a pleasant summit with a scattering of granite boulders. Keeping a course parallel with the north shore of the tarn, next visit Water Crag, passing a good specimen of the several ancient cairns in this vicinity, and then descend to cross the outlet of the tarn, Linbeck Gill, after which climb the grass slopes to the south, working to the right to a rocky ridge and the splendid columnar cairn on White Pike: a very fine viewpoint (note Muncaster Castle). Woodend Height, left, and Yoadcastle, right, are now seen side by side, waiting patiently to be climbed, a halfmile distant. Aim first for Yoadcastle, attaining its summit of naked rock by a stiff scramble and, when there, agreeing with the author that its altitude, although not officially triangulated, is obviously greater than that of Woodend Height. Then cross to the latter, drinking in the excellent view before making an easy mile-long beeline down to the boathouse, where the wide track is rejoined for the return to the car. But, if a flicker of energy remains in the old legs, deviate to the abrupt rock-tower of Seat How, nearby on the right, and try to find a way to its summit: no easy task, but on the east side a chink in its armour provides a passage to its airy crest and gives a good finish to the day's walk.

Seat How

MAP

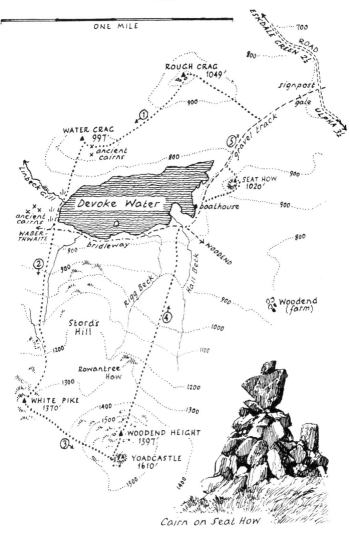

ONE MILE

ESKDALE GREEN 2½

ROAD

700

800

signpost

gate

ULPHA 3½

ROUGH CRAG
1049'

900

①

WATER CRAG
997'

×× ancient
cairns

800

⑤

gravel track

900

SEAT HOW
1020'

900

Lin beck Gill

Devoke Water

boathouse

×× ancient
cairns

←WABER-
THWAITE

bridleway

800

WOODEND

800

②

900

Rigg Beck

Hall Beck

900

Woodend
(farm)

Stord's
Hill

1000

1100

1200

Rowantree
How

1300

1200

1300

1200

▲WHITE PIKE
1370'

1400

1300

③

1500

▲WOODEND HEIGHT
1597'

YOADCASTLE
1610'

1500

1400

Cairn on Seat How

149

Stainton Pike

visiting
Stainton Pike, 1632'
The Knott, 1071'

1550 feet of ascent

from WABERTHWAITE

$8\frac{3}{4}$ miles

6 hours

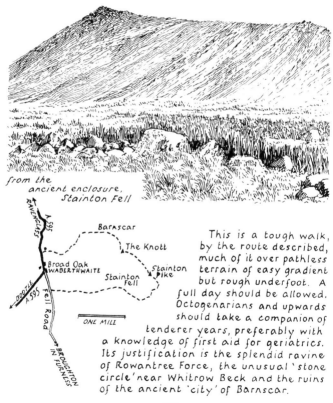

*from the
ancient enclosure,
Stainton Fell*

This is a tough walk, by the route described, much of it over pathless terrain of easy gradient but rough underfoot. A full day should be allowed. Octogenarians and upwards should take a companion of tenderer years, preferably with a knowledge of first aid for geriatrics. Its justification is the splendid ravine of Rowantree Force, the unusual 'stone circle' near Whitrow Beck and the ruins of the ancient 'city' of Barnscar.

150

Stainton Pike, one of the half-dozen well-defined summits on the long ridge extending from the top of the Fell Road in the south to Devoke Water, is a shapely and abrupt peak amongst low crags and boulders, and, with its uninterrupted outlook to the estuary of the Esk and the sea, viewed above a sharp downfall, is a pleasant halting place.

Below the steep decline of the western flank, a dreary moorland, interesting only for its relics of bygone civilisations, extends to the green fields of Waberthwaite. A new plantation has sprung from this desolation in recent years and the whole of Stainton Fell and its Pike are now imprisoned in a tight wire fence, a fetter quite out of keeping with the traditional freedom of fell country.

The best natural feature is an imposing ravine containing a fine double waterfall appropriately named Rowantree Force, which, being away from beaten tracks and hidden from sight until reached remains virtually unknown to fellwalkers.

Ancient cairn,
Stainton Fell

Rowantree Force

Summit cairn

Stainton Pike

Summit cairn

The Knott

Seen from the Knott, Stainton Pike (in the background) assumes the pyramidal shape of Bowfell, which, for so unpretentious a fell, is praise indeed. This is the best viewpoint for the Pike.

152

A long third of a mile up the Fell Road from its junction with the A.595 at Broad Oak, a rough access road turns off to Grange Farm. (There may, or may not, be a "Bridleway to Stainton Fell" sign at the corner). There is very limited parking space nearby on the verge of the Fell Road. Walk along the farm access as far as a facing gate at the end of the straight section, pass through it, cross Whitrow Beck after 200 yards and aim over the open moor on the north side of the beck. The bridleway already is barely distinguishable but the general direction is clear and the walking is easy. On a slight rise an area of antiquarian interest is reached: here are several old cairns and the parapet of a circular enclosure. The official bridleway now fords the beck and loops round the fellside, aiming for the depression in the skyline ahead but its route is not favoured because it misses a highlight of the journey —the spectacular ravine of Rowantree Force. To see this, continue forward and ascend the south rim of the ravine (the north side is fenced). Above a double waterfall that cries out to be photographed and poses perfectly for it, the gradient eases and the beck should be forded at any convenient place, to join the fence, which is then followed round onto the broad top of Stainton Fell. Don't attempt to climb the fence (which could have painful results) even though it seems to be trending off course; but persevere alongside until a gate in it is reached near Holehouse Tarn. From the gate it is a simple walk to the top of Stainton Pike, marked by a big cairn in a surround of crags and boulders. The next objective, the Knott, is seen across a wide hollow. Reach it by first circling round to the north to avoid rough ground. The damned fence is met again and this time will have to be climbed: protect your privates. Then make a beeline for the Knott, avoiding marshy patches. There is a tedious descent from the Knott north-west into a wide basin and a gentle slope beyond leads to the many relics of the ancient settlement of Barnscar: a hunting ground for archaeologists but unlikely to cause palpitation in the breast of the unlearned walker, whose gaze will be riveted more on the Coolin-like rugosities of the White Pike ridge. The remains of the settlement are profuse but obscured a great deal by bracken, as is the bridleway across the site promised by the Ordnance maps. In fact the bridleway, as far as the walled lane going down to Dyke Farm, can be written off as non-existent and time spent looking for it is time wasted, and at a cost of wet feet. Rather better is the so-called public footpath also indicated on Ordnance maps. In either case the walled lane is reached with relief, and can be followed down in pleasant surroundings, amid trees, to Dyke Farm and the main road A.595. Note, on the descent, an unusual tower crowning a steep bluff nearby to the north, but, with energy now flagging fast, any thought of visiting it must be banished. The mile of roadwalking needed to return to the parked car, much of it uphill, is a severe tax on the last vestiges of strength.

A map of the route is given overleaf ⟶

153

MAP

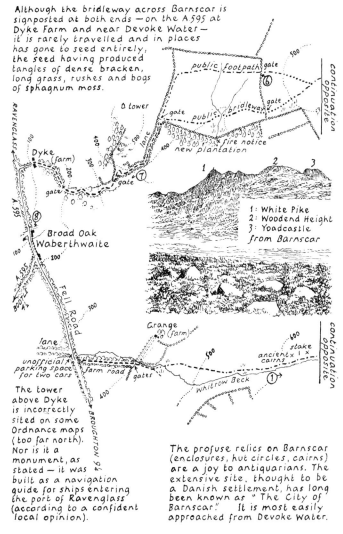

Although the bridleway across Barnscar is signposted at both ends — on the A595 at Dyke Farm and near Devoke Water — it is rarely travelled and in places has gone to seed entirely, the seed having produced tangles of dense bracken, long grass, rushes and bogs of sphagnum moss.

public footpath gate

500

continuation opposite

□ tower

gate public bridleway gate

lane

RAVENGLASS

100

400

300

100

200

fire notice

new plantation

Dyke (farm)

gate ⑦

gate

A.595

⑧

Broad Oak
Waberthwaite

100

200

BOOTLE A2

Fell Road

300

400

BROUGHTON 94

1: White Pike
2: Woodend Height
3: Yoadcastle
from Barnscar

lane

unofficial parking space for two cars

Grange (farm)

farm road

gates

500

ancient cairns × stake × ×

⑥

⑥

① →

continuation opposite

Whitrow Beck

600

The tower above Dyke is incorrectly sited on some Ordnance maps (too far north). Nor is it a monument, as stated — it was built as a navigation guide for ships entering the port of Ravenglass (according to a confident local opinion).

The profuse relics on Barnscar (enclosures, hut circles, cairns) are a joy to antiquarians. The extensive site, thought to be a Danish settlement, has long been known as "The City of Barnscar." It is most easily approached from Devoke Water.

154

MAP

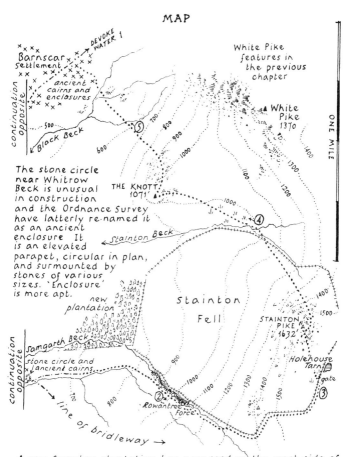

White Pike features in the previous chapter

DEVOKE WATER 1

Barnscar Settlement

ancient cairns and enclosures

White Pike 1370

500

Black Beck

600

700

800

900

1000

⑤

THE KNOTT 1071'

1100

1200

1300

1400

The stone circle near Whitrow Beck is unusual in construction and the Ordnance Survey have latterly re-named it as an ancient enclosure It is an elevated parapet, circular in plan, and surmounted by stones of various sizes. 'Enclosure' is more apt.

Stainton Beck

④

1000

new plantation

Stainton Fell

900

1000

1100

1200

1300

1400

1500

STAINTON PIKE 1632'

Samgarth Beck

stone circle and ancient cairns

700

800

⑦

Rowantree Force

Holehouse Tarn

gate

③

line of bridleway →

ONE MILE

A new forestry plantation has appeared on the west side of Stainton Fell. There can be little quarrel with this use of the ground, the area covered being formerly wasteland. But from the edge of the plantation has sprung a wiremesh fence with cruel barbs, enclosing the whole of Stainton Fell and its Pike, which, one presumes, marks the boundary of the area acquired by the Forestry Commission. Was this fence really necessary? Trees will never be planted so high! And was the barbing essential? Who is the enemy? And, if evidence of ownership by title deeds is not enough and must be indicated by a fence, wouldn't it have been rather thoughtful to have provided a few step-stiles? The walkers were here first!

Whit Fell

visiting
Buck Barrow, 1799'
Whit Fell, 1881'
Burn Moor, 1780'
Kinmont Buck Barrow, 1754'

1100 feet of ascent

from THE FELL ROAD

5 3/4 miles

3 hours

On Ordnance maps
Whit Fell appears
as Whitfell
(one word)

Whit Fell,
from
Buck Barrow

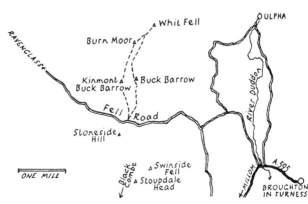

OULPHA

Whit Fell

Burn Moor

RAVENGLASS

Kinmont
Buck Barrow

Buck Barrow

River Duddon

Fell Road

Stoneside
Hill

ONE MILE

Black
Combe

Swinside
Fell

Stoupdale
Head

MILLOM

A.595

BROUGHTON
IN FURNESS

156

The high mass of Black Combe extends northwards in an undulating skyline with little loss of elevation to merge with the greater fells of Lakeland around the headwaters of the Esk and the Duddon. The culmination of this extensive upland is Whit Fell, not much lower than Black Combe itself and little inferior as a viewpoint. Apart from the rocky crest of Buck Barrow the range is unexciting, a vast sheep pasture more Pennine than Lakeland in character and appearing all the bleaker because of the contrast with its lovely enclosing valleys. Consequently this is an unfrequented region (except for Devoke Water) but it is good walking country unimpeded by fences, and its demerits are fully compensated by the excellence of the views.

The summit cairn,
Kinmont Buck Barrow

In this book the main summits of the Whit Fell range are described as separate walks, but the ideal way of visiting them is by a single traverse from the Fell Road to Devoke Water if transport can be arranged at both ends. Walkers who do this will enjoy a fine expedition, neither too long (6½ miles) nor too arduous (1200 feet of ascent). They will not rate it with the popular Lakeland ridgewalks but may well consider it the best high-level approach to the central mountains. Developing this idea, note that one may walk over the tops all the way from the sea to Crinkle Crags, between the Esk and Duddon valleys: a perfect entrance, but not, alas, a route for veterans.

Buck Barrow

top: *Buckbarrow Crag*

middle:
  the lower summit

right:
  the rock turret

Whit Fell

left:
the summit cairn

middle:
looking south
from the summit

bottom:
looking to the
Coniston Fells
from the summit

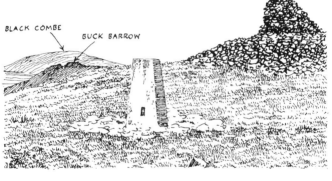

BLACK COMBE

BUCK BARROW

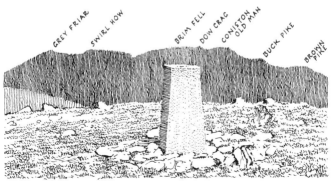

GREY FRIAR

SWIRL HOW

BRIM FELL

DOW CRAG

CONISTON OLD MAN

BUCK PIKE

BROWN PIKE

Start the walk from the summit of the Fell Road, using a grassy cart-track alongside the wall heading northeast, and keeping to this until it turns away below the rocks of Buck Barrow. Then aim for the nearest top, reaching it by a short scramble after crossing an encircling band of grey boulders. A second and higher top is now revealed: pass to it below a rock turret, crossing more boulders here and climbing amongst low crags to the highest point. Buck Barrow is attractively adorned with bristly pinnacles, some of which, when we were lads, we would have been tempted to climb. Its appearance from a distance mildly resembles Stac Polly; it is the finest summit in the Black Combe area. There is nothing as good beyond and no need to go further unless more exercise is wanted, in which case descend the far slope and aim across tedious and uninteresting grass, contouring the slopes of Burn Moor, to the prominent cairn on Whit Fell. The final incline is relieved by outcrops and the summit is pleasant. It is crowned by a great heap of stones, apparently a tumulus, out of which the massive cairn has been fashioned. An Ordnance column (S.5472) stands on grass on the north-east side.

Whit Fell is a superb viewpoint, the panorama including the Duddon and Esk estuaries, the Isle of Man, the coastal plain to St. Bees Head and an uninterrupted range of peaks with the Pillar, Scafell, Bowfell and Coniston groups well displayed beyond the upper reaches of Wasdale, Eskdale and the Duddon Valley.

Return by way of the summit of Burn Moor, not because of any merit it has but merely for a variation of route. A beeline can then be made for the wall seen running up to the rocky crest of Kinmont Buck Barrow, crossing a shallow depression with peat hags. Kinmont's abrupt top, a stony headland with a fine seaward view, is delightful. Avoid crags by descending on the west side and then aim over easy grass, crossing broken walls, to the waiting car.

The summit of Burn Moor, looking south to
Buck Barrow, Black Combe and Kinmont Buck Barrow.

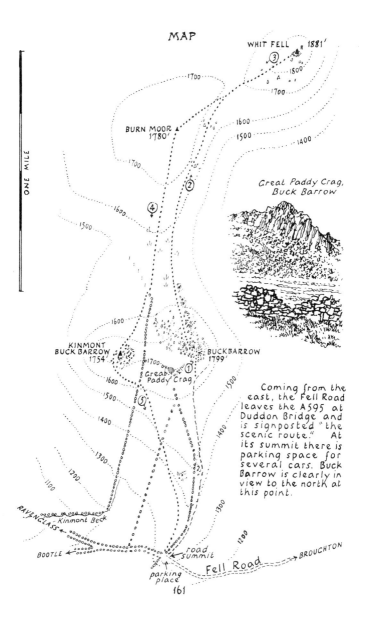

MAP

WHIT FELL 1881'
③

1700

1800

1700

BURN MOOR
1780'

1600

1500

1400

1700

②

Great Paddy Crag,
Buck Barrow

④

1600

1500

1600

KINMONT
BUCK BARROW
1754'

1700

①

BUCKBARROW
1799'

Great
Paddy Crag

1600

1500

1500

⑤

1400

1400

1300

1300

1200

Coming from the
east, the Fell Road
leaves the A595 at
Duddon Bridge and
is signposted "the
scenic route." At
its summit there is
parking space for
several cars. Buck
Barrow is clearly in
view to the north at
this point.

1100

1200

RAVENGLASS
Kinmont Beck

BOOTLE

road
summit

1200

BROUGHTON

parking
place

Fell Road

ONE MILE

161

Black Combe

We were brought up to believe that
the height of Black Combe was 1969'.
The Ordnance Survey have latterly
been suffering agonies of doubt and
now announce the altitude as

1970'

Well, let's have it right.

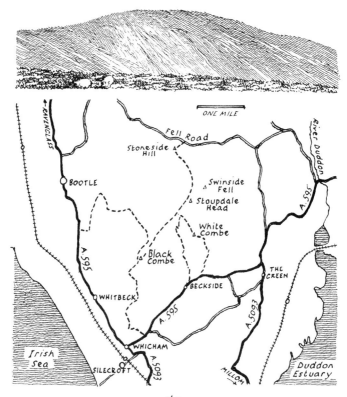

Visitors to Lakeland, especially if newly introduced to the district, often have difficulty in identifying many of the mountains by name, even distinctive ones such as Great Gable and Bowfell and Pillar assuming different shapes from unfamiliar angles. But Black Combe is never confused with others. Although in fact linked with the main grouping of high fells by a continuous ridge it appears aloof, rising on the southern seaboard and overtopping all else like a huge whale stranded on a beach, a landmark visible over far distances and always unmistakeable. Because of its detachment Black Combe is rarely included by fellwalking visitors in their itineraries, yet is within the boundary of the National Park, which hereabouts coincides with the shoreline, and its ascent, in conditions of clear visibility, is one of the most rewarding. As a viewpoint it is unique. Half of the panorama is the glittering sea, with the Isle of Man seen in stark outline and Wales, Ireland and Scotland as shadowy silhouettes on a high horizon of water. A fine array of mountains is the landward feature, the fells of southern Lakeland ranging across the scene and appearing, at this distance, in correct perspective, while round to the east the Pennines and the Bowland Fells form the background to a colourful landscape of undulating terrain pierced by long estuaries and dotted with scattered small towns and villages. The coast is seen, an unbroken line, from St. Bees Head to the Isle of Walney.

Black Combe and its satellites form a lofty mass between the valleys of the Duddon and the Esk. A single-track road and a few paths cross this wild upland. It is excellent territory for walking, with enough possible variations of routes to cater for a full week afoot.

Black Combe was made to be climbed, and climbed it should be. It is considerate to the old and infirm: the grass bridleway to its summit from Whicham is amongst the most delectable of Lakeland fell paths. Which other can be ascended in carpet slippers ?

The start of the Whicham path
as seen from the church

Site of old copper mine,
Whitecombe Beck

The Whicham path at 1500'

right:
    Whitecombe
        Screes

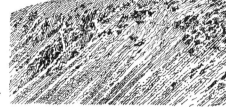

below:
    Whicham Mill

Three routes of ascent are described, with maps, in the following pages: from south, west and north, the first two being on excellent continuous paths; and a fourth, from the east (via White Combe), is suggested. A defect of the first three is the lack of alternative routes of return to the startingpoint for walkers whose base is a parked car, but if use can be made of bus or train services or if a mutual arrangement can be made with another party of like ambition to exchange cars parked at different places, then a combination of routes is possible.

Allow four hours for any of the three direct routes (up and down) but more on days of clear visibility.

ASCENT FROM WHICHAM

1900 feet of ascent including detours

5¼ miles
there and back

The ascent of Black Combe from Whicham is the route most favoured, is without complications, and much the best: indeed the splendid path that directs the feet upwards to the very top, and the unparalleled views, make it a classic. The climb is unremitting, although easing midway, so that the amount of ascent between Whicham at 120 feet and the summit at 1970 is exactly 1850 feet, no more and no less; and the well-contrived cart-width path of dry turf makes every inch a delight. This path is not only the best way up but also the best way down and is recommended for use both ways with little detours on the summit. Walkers who object to treading the same ground twice can combine the route with one of the other three given, but in this case the Whicham path should be reserved for descent.

Surprisingly, the start of this popular climb is without a signpost. The church is the clue. Adjacent is the school, now closed. Park the car unobtrusively in the schoolyard (which still has functional toilets for boys and girls adaptable for grown-ups also) and proceed on the tarmac lane alongside to the farm at its end, rounding the buildings by a walled track to the open fell. Cross a new wire fence here (stile) and join and follow the grass path slanting up to the right. It would take a genius to go astray now. The path winds up unmistakeably, occasionally being bypassed where overgrown, and climbs to the top of the side-valley of Moorgill Beck, at 1000 feet, where the upper slopes of the fell come into view with the path seen slanting left across the heathery dome above exposures of pink scree. Extensive vistas east and west, ranging from the Pennines to the Isle of Man, also appear as the path continues, now less steeply. Higher, at 1850 feet, the path forks, one branch skirting the summit and the other climbing directly to the top. At this point turn up right onto the south shoulder for the prospect seawards before proceeding to the Ordnance column on the main top. A short detour eastwards to see Blackcombe Screes is recommended. Return along the same path, again enjoying the fine views that endow Black Combe with a distinction not shared by other Lakeland fells.

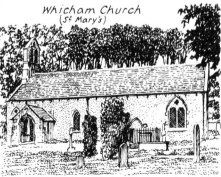

Whicham Church
(St Mary's)

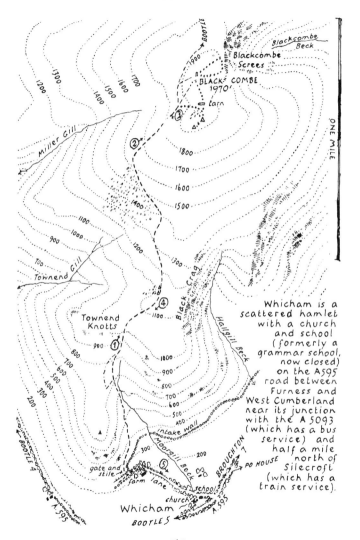

Whicham is a scattered hamlet with a church and school (formerly a grammar school, now closed) on the A595 road between Furness and West Cumberland near its junction with the A5093 (which has a bus service) and half a mile north of Silecroft (which has a train service).

ASCENT FROM HOLEGILL BRIDGE, BOOTLE
1950 feet of ascent
8 miles there and back

The bridleway up the western flank provides another well-graded and distinct route to the summit of Black Combe, easier even than the Whicham path but longer and more circuitous.

A bridleway runs along the western base of Black Combe by the intake wall and parallel to the main road. Reaching it from the road out of Bootle appears to be legitimate only at one point: by public footpath 300 yards south of Holegill Bridge at a gate directly opposite a lane to Barfield and adjacent to a tree-shadowed ruin where there is parking space for two cars (there is better parking north of the bridge). The walk is deemed to start here and miles are measured on the map from this point. Unfortunately the gate is barricaded and in the absence of a stile must be climbed — this is a matter the Barrow Ramblers might care to take up with the farmer. From the gate a track goes alongside a wall and emerges, over another 'closed' gate, onto the bridleway. Now all is plain sailing. Turn left, cross a beck, and follow the intake wall to the ruins of Hall Foss, where the bridleway turns uphill by a wall succeeded by a fence, swinging to the right on the brow of the hill (view forward here to the Pillar range). The only further direction necessary is to keep the bridleway underfoot:

STOP PRESS!
Starting gate now cleared and footpath sign erected.

it is grassy, of cart width, provides simple walking, and, although circuitous, cleverly avoiding all depressions, leads unerringly to the top of Black Combe (and continues thence down to Whicham). The surroundings on this ascent are tedious but relieved by the distant views. On the summit, which is left of the path, visit the rim of the Screes, and, if visibility is good, the lower south top.

The finest descent, unquestionably, is down the bridleway to Whicham, and this is where the non-car-owner scores if he can arrange his times to catch a bus back to Bootle. Otherwise return by the route of ascent. A short cut by William Gill and Holegill Beck, saving a mile, is obvious, but the walking, through lush pastures of bilberry, and lower down steep bracken, is slow compared with the bridleway, along which a spanking pace can be worked up and the car reached in an hour although a leisurely saunter is preferable.

168

MAP

ONE MILE

A more convenient start and finish to the walk would be along the farm lane to Hall Foss, but this is severely gated (five times) and is not a right of way.

Aeroplane wreckage is scattered about the higher western slopes and occurs also in the valley of Blackcombe Beck, east of the summit.

700
800
900
1000
1100
1200
1300
1400
1500
1600
1700

Hentoe Beck

fold x
② ⑥

Hallfoss Beck

Little Fell

700
800
900
1000
1100
1200

Holegill Beck

William Gill

⑤ ③
1700

1500
1600
1700
1800

Blackcombe Screes

BLACK COMBE
1970'

tarn
④
south top

WHICHAM

Ruins of Hall Foss

continuation opposite

ASCENT FROM THE FELL ROAD
1350 feet of ascent

7 miles
there and back

Ancient limbs will respond more readily to the route to Black Combe from the top of the fell road, this, at 1300 feet, giving a good 'leg up' for walkers with cars, and the climbing, furthermore, being of easy gradient. It is, however, a tedious approach and rather marred by a bad swamp that must be faced twice, there being no alternative way back to the car. But if a plan can be devised for sending the car round to await you at Whicham Church or arrangements made for a mutual exchange of cars with someone of like ambition, this line of ascent combined with a descent to Whicham makes a splendid traverse of Black Combe from end to end.

There is carparking space at the summit of the fell road on the south side. Black Combe is in view here, to the left of the prominent Stoneside Hill, a rough little eminence crossed by a wall. This is the first objective. On the far side there is an unfortunate loss of height to a swamp in a depression. Cross it gingerly; wet feet are inevitable. Then climb the easy slope beyond, keeping a line of old fence posts in sight and so arrive on the indefinite top of Stoupdale Head. (A short detour left here brings the valley of Stoupdale into view directly below, and away to the left in the next valley, the stone circle at Swinside can be discerned).

Black Combe looms ahead. Aim for it across a depression and follow the edge of Whitecombe Screes and Blackcombe Screes, above a deep valley on the left, to the summit. If time and energy permit, visit the south top also. Failing a car-swap with a friend coming up from Whicham (whose arrival on the summit should coincide with yours), return to the fell road by the same route, deviating only to skirt round the top of Stoneside Hill.

Stoupdale Head and Black Combe, from Stoneside Hill

170

MAP

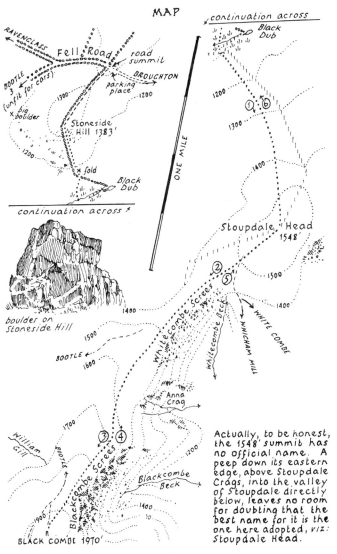

continuation across →

RAVENGLASS

Fell Road

road summit

BROUGHTON

parking place

BOOTLE 3 (unfit for cars)

big × boulder

1300

1200

Stoneside Hill 1383'

1200

× fold

Black Dub

continuation across ↗

boulder on Stoneside Hill

ONE MILE

Black Dub

1200

1300

① ⑥

1400

Stoupdale Head 1548

② ⑤

1500

1400

WHITE COMBE

WHICHAM MILL

Whitecombe Screes

Whitecombe Beck

1400

1500

BOOTLE ←

1600

Anna Crag

1200

1700

William Gill

1800

③ ④

Blackcombe Screes

Blackcombe Beck

1900

1400

BLACK COMBE 1970'

Actually, to be honest, the 1548' summit has no official name. A peep down its eastern edge, above Stoupdale Crags, into the valley of Stoupdale directly below, leaves no room for doubting that the best name for it is the one here adopted, viz: Stoupdale Head.

171

ASCENT OF WHITE COMBE FROM BECKSIDE
1250 feet of ascent

4½ miles
3 hours

White Combe is a buttress of Black Combe on the east side, separated by a valley but with a high-level link. It makes a fine walk, returning down the valley, and can conveniently be used as a stepping-stone to its bigger neighbour.

From its junction with the side-road to Ralliss go along the A595 east for a third of a mile until, on a bend, a gated lane between hedges branches off on the left: it is a public footpath but has the appearance of a virgin jungle. A safari along it leads to a gate giving access to the open fell, a sea of bracken, which is bisected by a deep groove (a drove road) slanting up to the right: a track runs alongside. Follow this. Beyond a zig-zag it becomes indistinct on easier ground, then re-appears to skirt the slopes of White Combe, the summit of which is reached by a simple climb up to the left and found to be crowned with a great heap of stones like a tumulus and fashioned into a wind-shelter. Then, for an alternative route of return, aim northwest along the level ridge to meet another drove road descending into the deep valley on the left. Follow this down, enjoying intimate views of the rough recesses of Black Combe and passing two heaps of spoil remaining from copper-mine operations, to the intake wall at the foot of the valley, where a track in pleasant wooded surroundings leads down to Whicham Mill (now an attractive cottage) and, becoming a tarmac road, continues past Ralliss to the A595.

The summit of White Combe
looking to Stoupdale Head

MAP

For a continuation of the map northwards see page 171

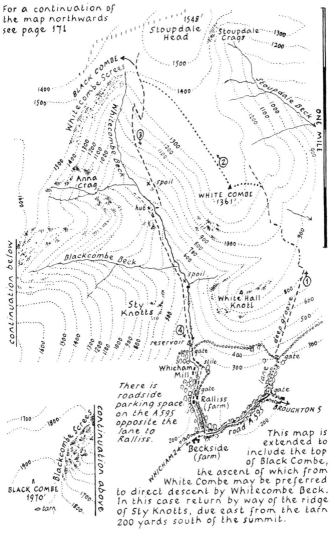

1548'
Stoupdale Head

Stoupdale Crags

1300
1200

1500

BLACK COMBE

Whitecombe Screes

Stoupdale Beck

1400
1500

1400

1100
1200

ONE MILE

900

③

1300
1200

②

Anna Crag

Whitecombe Beck

x spoil

WHITE COMBE
1361'

hut

1300
1200

1000

1000

Blackcombe Beck

800
700
600

1000

spoil

900

deep groove

①

800

600
500

Sty Knotts

White Hall Knott

400

300

continuation below

④

reservoir

gate
stile
300

400

gate

300

lane

gate

Whicham Mill

200

gate

Ralliss (farm)

gate

BROUGHTON 5

There is roadside parking space on the A595 opposite the lane to Ralliss.

WHICHAM

Beckside (farm)

A595 road

200

This map is extended to include the top of Black Combe, the ascent of which from White Combe may be preferred to direct descent by Whitecombe Beck. In this case return by way of the ridge of Sty Knotts, due east from the tarn 200 yards south of the summit.

continuation above

Blackcombe Screes

1700
1800
1900

BLACK COMBE
1970'

tarn

1700
1800

The summit, a beacon site, is a smooth grassy plateau, so flat that the Ordnance column and its walled surround cannot be seen until the last few moments of ascent; in fact there are football grounds with playing surfaces a lot worse than the top of Black Combe. A short stroll eastwards leads to the striking downfall of Blackcombe Screes, a steep craggy declivity forming the mountain's best feature. South of the main summit and beyond a depression containing a tarn is a stonier subsidiary top, which has well-built cairns indicating better viewpoints for the extensive seascape and coastline.

Just to make sure you have climbed the right fell check the number of the Ordnance column. If it is 2953 your orienteering has been impeccable.

POSTSCRIPT, added in 1979:

No, not now 2953. The column was rebuilt in 1976 after vandalism, the new number being 11602.

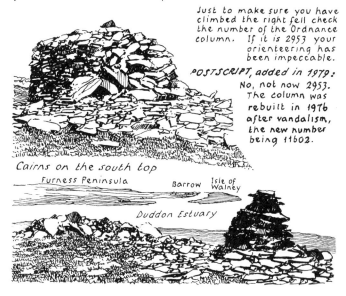

Cairns on the south top

Furness Peninsula   Barrow   Isle of Walney

Duddon Estuary

Blackcombe Screes

above: *looking north to Buck Barrow*
            and Whitfell
below: *looking south*

THE VIEW

The Lakeland Skyline

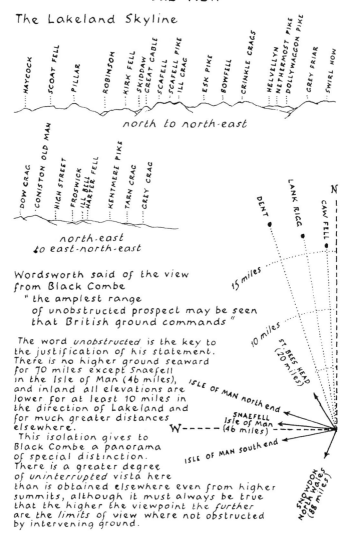

north to north-east

MAYCOCK · SCOAT FELL · PILLAR · ROBINSON · KIRK FELL · SKIDDAW · GREAT GABLE · SCAFELL · SCAFELL PIKE · ILL CRAG · ESK PIKE · BOWFELL · CRINKLE CRAGS · HELVELLYN · NETHERMOST PIKE · DOLLYWAGGON PIKE · GREY FRIAR · SWIRL HOW

north-east to east-north-east

DOW CRAG · CONISTON OLD MAN · HIGH STREET · FROSWICK · ILL BELL · HARTER FELL · KENTMERE PIKE · TARN CRAG · GREY CRAG

Wordsworth said of the view from Black Combe

" the amplest range of unobstructed prospect may be seen that British ground commands "

The word *unobstructed* is the key to the justification of his statement. There is no higher ground seaward for 70 miles except Snaefell in the Isle of Man (46 miles), and inland all elevations are lower for at least 10 miles in the direction of Lakeland and for much greater distances elsewhere.

This isolation gives to Black Combe a panorama of special distinction. There is a greater degree of uninterrupted vista here than is obtained elsewhere even from higher summits, although it must always be true that the higher the viewpoint the *further* are the *limits* of view where not obstructed by intervening ground.

N

DENT · LANK RIGG · CAW FELL

15 miles

10 miles

ST. BEES HEAD (20 miles)

ISLE OF MAN north end

SNAEFELL Isle of Man (46 miles)

W

ISLE OF MAN south end

SNOWDON NORTH WALES (88 miles)

176

The high ground of Lakeland fits neatly into the sector between north (map north not magnetic north) and east-north-east. The array of mountains is splendid but is confined almost entirely to those in the southern part of the district. As a viewpoint of Lakeland Black Combe is much inferior to many other elevations, Skiddaw Little Man (the best of all) for instance. Nevertheless the prospect is one of great charm, the Esk and Duddon valleys leading the eye to a concentration of noble peaks.

Principal Fells

SKIDDAW

N

HELVELLYN
NETHERMOST PIKE
DOLLYWAGGON PIKE

25 miles

HIGH STREET

ROBINSON

HAYCOCK
SCOAT FELL
PILLAR

KIRK FELL
GREAT GABLE
SCAFELL
SCAFELL PIKE
ILL CRAG
ESK PIKE
BOWFELL
CRINKLE CRAGS

20 miles

ILL BELL
HARTER FELL

KENTMERE PIKE
TARN CRAG
GREY CRAG

GREY FRIAR
SWIRL HOW

BUCK BARROW
WHITFELL
HESK FELL
GREEN CRAG
WHITE
STICKLE
CAW

DOW CRAG
CONISTON OLD MAN

WOODLAND FELL
TOP O' SELSIDE

BLAWITH KNOTT

GUMMER'S HOW

BURNEY

E

INGLEBOROUGH (38 miles)

BARROW IN FURNESS
ISLE OF WALNEY

As a place for appraising the coastal plain and estuaries, however, Black Combe is quite supreme. Thirty continuous miles of shoreline and its pleasant hinterland are seen as on a map. The towns and villages fit unobtrusively into a tranquil scene. The one jarring feature is the atomic power station, spoiling the prospect of the Esk estuary and the sands of Ravenglass.

177

Boat How
1105'

1000 feet of ascent

from BOOT

4 miles

2½ hours

The ridge of which Boat How is the summit separates the upper reaches of Miterdale and a wide depression draining into Eskdale. It stands on the fringe of some of the finest mountain terrain in the district, being almost within the shadow of Scafell, and a popular path runs along its eastern flank, but because of the greater appeal of the higher fells the summit is rarely visited, and, truth to tell, there is nothing here to compete with its better-known neighbours.

In one respect, however, is this ridge unique. Its proliferation of ancient remains makes it a happy hunting ground for walkers with an eye for relics of days long past. A remarkable concentration of such monuments includes four stone circles.

178

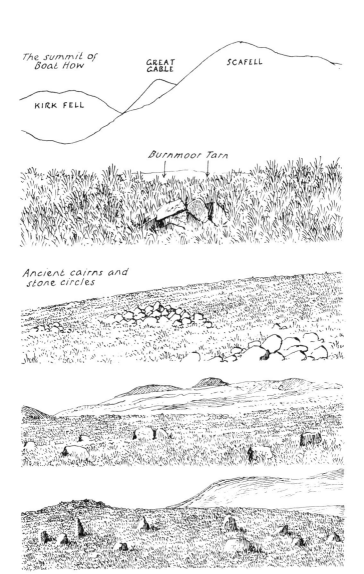

The summit of
Boat How

KIRK FELL

GREAT
GABLE

SCAFELL

Burnmoor Tarn

Ancient cairns and
stone circles

Harter Fell, Great Barrow
and Little Barrow,
from Gill Bank,

The walk starts from Boot along the popular bridleway to
Wasdale Head via Burnmoor Tarn, leaving the village over the
bridge by the old mill and passing through an often-opened gate
to a much-trodden path ascending half-right. Leave this after
150 yards by a gate in the wall on the right. The route is now
clear, keeping the contour through several gated enclosures
and continuing beyond across the open moor. When abreast
of a stone hut 100 yards on the left turn to it and continue
in the same direction up a gentle slope, crossing a shepherd's
track midway, to the conspicuous top of Boat How, an abrupt
rocky oasis in a prairie of long grass. From the small cairn
the far shore of Burnmoor Tarn is in view backed by a massive
Scafell with Kirk Fell and Great Gable to its left; Miterdale is
seen full length and Harter Fell and Green Crag form a skyline
of considerable attraction. Aim now along the pathless ridge
southwest, parallel with Miterdale, for half a mile to an area
of ancient cairns with a stone circle, proceeding thence south
to another collection of antiquities including three more stone
circles and innumerable old cairns. After an exploration of this
impressive site, walk east to join a track that descends past
the ruins of Gill Bank and goes down to Boot between walls.

MAP

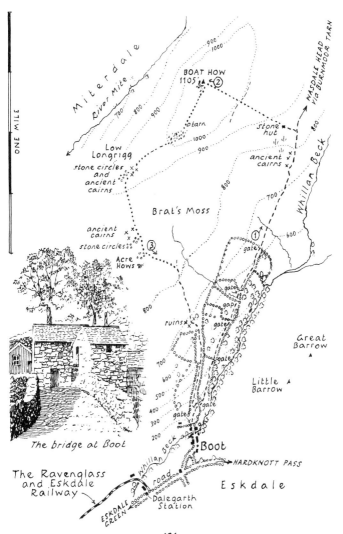

One Mile

Miterdale

River Mire

900
1000
700
800
900

BOAT HOW
1105 ②

MASDALE HEAD via BURNMOOR TARN

tarn

stone hut

Low Longrigg
stone circles and ancient cairns

1000

900

ancient cairns

800

Brat's Moss

800

700

Whillan Beck

600

ancient cairns
stone circles

③

①

gate

Acre Hows

800

gate

gate

gap

ruins

gate

700

600

500

gate

Great Barrow

Little Barrow

400

300

gates

gate

200

Boot

HARDKNOTT PASS

The bridge at Boot

The Ravenglass and Eskdale Railway

Whillan Beck

road

ESKDALE GREEN

Dalegarth Station

Eskdale

181

Irton Pike
751'

830 feet of ascent

from IRTON ROAD
RAILWAY STATION

5¼ miles

3 hours

Travelling inland on the miniature railway from Ravenglass on the coast the first prominent rise on the skyline across the flat fields of Miterdale is a low shapely summit standing naked above a dense cloak of woodland and plantations. This is Irton Pike, the abrupt terminus of a long ridge descending from the heights above Wastwater, and a delectable objective in its own right but no longer easily accessible because of growing timber, and which might be completely isolated and unattainable in a few years' time as trees mature. Its view seawards is unrestricted but the gem of a wide panorama is Great Gable — a noble sight at the head of Wasdale. Couches of lovely heather make this tiny top a near-perfect solace for reminiscences of past happy days on the higher fells. Climb Irton Pike while ye may!

182

The Ravenglass and Eskdale Railway
(affectionately known as "La'al Ratty")

Dating from 1875, the Ravenglass and Eskdale Railway was originally laid on a 3-foot gauge for the transport of iron ore from the mines of Boot to the coast, and, after many vicissitudes and closure in 1913 the line was subsequently revived and relaid on a 15" gauge for the transport of passengers and goods, mainly granite from the Beckfoot quarries; but with the closure of the quarries the railway was sold by auction in 1960 and acquired by a group of railway enthusiasts, who, to their credit, operate it most efficiently. The line is a great attraction and the Ravenglass terminus presents an animated and busy scene in complete contrast with the British Railways station adjoining, which is unstaffed and shabby.

The Ravenglass and Eskdale Railway Preservation Society have given British Railways an object lesson on how to run a railway.

Admittedly, these illustrations have nothing to do with the Outlying fells. Makes a nice change from drawing mountains, though.

The royal way to arrive for an expedition to Irton Pike is by the miniature railway to Irton Road Station, four miles out of Ravenglass. A lane leads from the station to the Eskdale Green road, along which turn left for 100 yards and then follow a minor road branching off to the right (for Miterdale Head, but not signposted), passing a new school and a complex of buildings occupying the site of a former mill to reach a sign on the left announcing a public bridleway to Irton Fell 1 and Wasdale 3. This is the path to take, and it is a charmer. A stone bridge over the River Mite is crossed at once and then the path adopts a sinuous course uphill in natural woodland to emerge on more open ground among scattered new plantations and abundant heather. The path is generally easy to follow: if in doubt at junctions keep going uphill. After a mile the ridge of Irton Fell is reached at a gate in a forest fence and the path to Wasdale goes forward; but here turn left, alongside a wall and descending slightly, in the direction of Irton Pike, seen now below eye-level and in a surround of trees. Aim for a gate in the enclosing fence but before reaching it turn aside to a massive heap of stones, which calls for investigation but offers no reason for being there. None the wiser, follow the fence to the right (do NOT pass through the gate) to a step-stile giving access to a sketchy track that leads directly between conifers to the bald top of the Pike. The descent on the south side is rough and steep: a thin track goes down into a jungle of trees and must be kept underfoot. Desperation is relieved when a forest access is crossed and a few yards further one steps upon the tarmac of the Santon Bridge road at Malkinson's monument, notes the last line of the inscription thereon, which assumes a sinister significance after the ordeals of the last few minutes, and, with a feeling of deliverance, turns left along the road to return to Irton Road Station and enjoy even more another ride on the train.

RED PIKE   YEWBARROW   KIRK FELL   GREAT GABLE   WHIN RIGG

Wasdale Head, from Irton Pike

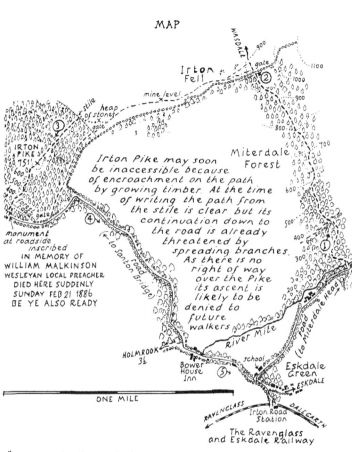

MAP

WASDALE

900

Irton Fell

gate

1100

1000

900

800

700

mine level

heap of stones

gate

stile

IRTON PIKE 751'

Miterdale Forest

600

500

400

300

200

Irton Pike may soon be inaccessible because of encroachment on the path by growing timber. At the time of writing the path from the stile is clear but its continuation down to the road is already threatened by spreading branches. As there is no right of way over the Pike its ascent is likely to be denied to future walkers

monument at roadside inscribed
IN MEMORY OF
WILLIAM MALKINSON
WESLEYAN LOCAL PREACHER
DIED HERE SUDDENLY
SUNDAY FEB 21 1886
BE YE ALSO READY

(to Santon Bridge)

(to Miterdale Head)

River Mite

HOLMROOK 3½

Bower House Inn

school

Eskdale Green

ESKDALE

ONE MILE

RAVENGLASS

Irton Road Station

DALEGARTH

The Ravenglass and Eskdale Railway

"... a massive heap of stones calls for investigation...."

What is its purpose, if any?
It is not a tumulus.
It is not a cairn.
It is not a wall.
It is not a bield.
It is not indicated on Ordnance maps.
It has an air of permanence but not of antiquity.
It could be nothing more than a collection of stones cleared from the adjacent forest in the course of planting.

185

Muncaster Fell

Hooker Crag 757'

750 feet of ascent

Not named on some editions
of the 1" Ordnance map.

from
**MUNCASTER CASTLE
CAR PARK**

7¼ miles

5 hours

Hooker Crag

Muncaster Fell is a lowly height that yet contrives to give an impression of much greater stature, especially when viewed from the miniature railway along its base where the rough craggy flank seems unassailable. Its situation, isolated between the flats of Miterdale and Eskdale, is magnificent, commanding a panorama of great charm both seawards and inland to the mountains of Lakeland. Heather and bilberry, gorse and bracken, woodland and forest, lay a rich carpet of colour over its slopes. But the supreme joy of Muncaster Fell is the delectable traverse of its ridge, as described in the pages following. Here is enchantment.

Muncaster Castle

Muncaster Castle, situated on a wooded hill enjoying a lovely view of Eskdale that inspired Ruskin to describe it as "the gateway to Paradise", occupies the location of a Roman tower, and dates from the 13th. century although extensively enlarged in more recent times. Its gardens are renowned for their exotic rhododendrons, camellias and azaleas. It is the seat of the Pennington family.

The summit of Muncaster Fell

Ross's Camp

Despite its name and its neolithic appearance this miniature man-made Stonehenge has no military or archaeological significance. It is a monument only to the physical strength of members of a Victorian shooting party who raised the massive flat slab onto other stones to serve as a luncheon table. The top of the slab is neatly inscribed ROSS'S CAMP 1883.

Miterdale and Scafell from Muncaster Fell

There is a large car-park opposite the main entrance to Muncaster Castle (provided free for the use of visitors to the Castle). From it walk Bootlewards along the A595 past a school and up a 1-in-5 rise to a sharp angle in the road, where two bridleways leave in the corner. Take the one signposted "Eskdale and Hardknott": this starts as a good straight cart-track up a leafy avenue between walls and rampant vegetation. Ignore a gated path branching off to the right at a fire notice. A depression is reached in a rhododendron grove and a half-hidden tarn amid trees is glimpsed as the track resumes its uphill journey to a gate in a fence, where a fine view unfolds. Directly ahead is seen the Ordnance column on Hooker Crag, with the Pillar group to its left and Scafell, Bowfell and Co. to its right. The Atomic Power Station is also unfortunately in sight northwest beyond the edge of a stand of mature Noble Fir. The track goes forward under a line of pylons with a new fence (enclosing a young plantation) alongside on the left: when this turns away a thin trod branches off the bridleway and leads pleasantly to the Ordnance column (NO. S.5763) in a sea of lovely heather. The view is now extensive and uninterrupted by higher ground: it ranges from the Isle of Man to Black Combe, the skyline including the Pillar, Scafell, Bowfell and Coniston groups. The thin trod descends beyond the column to cross a flat depression and peters out below another summit of lush heather and bilberry: here cross wet ground to the right to rejoin the bridleway, now less distinct but marked by standing stones. A large flat boulder supported by others is reached: this is Ross's Camp, another fine viewpoint with a charming prospect of Miterdale and Eskdale. Beyond, the bridleway swings left to a gate in a wall-corner and then continues downhill (rather wet), inclining across a depression on the right. A slight rise is followed by a long descent, the path here being retained by a granite wall. A stile in a crosswall ahead is used to continue forward in a surround of rich vegetation to another wall and a gate. A cart-track here goes down to the farm of Muncaster Head: pass through three gates to the right of the buildings to reach the farm access lane. Turn right along this for 1½ pleasantly wooded miles to High Eskholme, where tarmac appears, and, a furlong beyond, leave it at a gap on the right, which admits to a bridleway rising indistinctly on a terrace of thick bracken with a wall on the left. Either follow this bridleway to rejoin the outward route at the tarn or, preferably, when buildings and an unusual tower are seen over the wall on the left, pass through a gate to them and join a lane that goes forward to the A595 exactly opposite the entrance to Muncaster Church and the nursery gardens of the Castle, both well worth a visit if time permits, and perhaps one should really pay 20 pence to enter the Castle grounds, having made use of the car-park. If no such moral obligation is felt, simply turn right along the A595 to the car.

A map of the route is given overleaf →

189

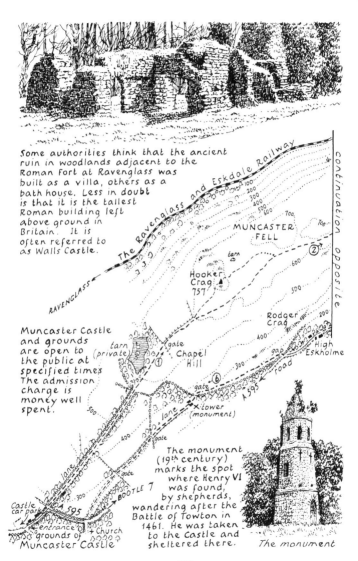

Some authorities think that the ancient ruin in woodlands adjacent to the Roman fort at Ravenglass was built as a villa, others as a bath house. Less in doubt is that it is the tallest Roman building left above ground in Britain. It is often referred to as Walls Castle.

The Ravenglass and Eskdale Railway

continuation opposite

RAVENGLASS

MUNCASTER FELL

tarn

Hooker Crag 757

Rodger Crag

High Eskholme

Muncaster Castle and grounds are open to the public at specified times. The admission charge is money well spent.

tarn (private)

gate ①

Chapel Hill

gate ⑥

A595 road

②

X tower (monument)

lane

gate

gate

BOTLLE 7

Castle car park

A595

entrance to grounds of Muncaster Castle

Church

The monument (19th century) marks the spot where Henry VI was found, by shepherds, wandering after the Battle of Towton in 1461. He was taken to the Castle and sheltered there.

The monument

190

MAP

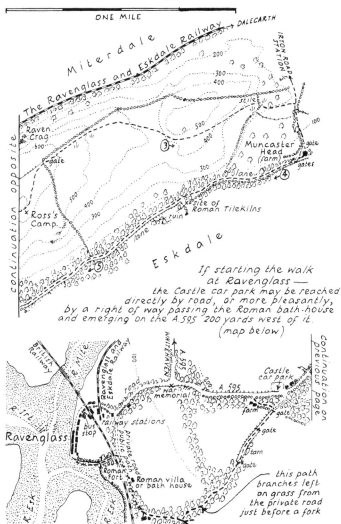

ONE MILE

Miterdale

The Ravenglass and Eskdale Railway → DALECARTH

IRTON ROAD STATION

stile

Raven Crag

③

P-gate

Muncaster Head (farm)

gate

gates

④

lane

continuation opposite

Ross's Camp.

site of Roman Tilekilns

ruin

lane

⑤

Eskdale

If starting the walk at Ravenglass —
the Castle car park may be reached
directly by road, or more pleasantly,
by a right of way passing the Roman bath-house
and emerging on the A.595 200 yards west of it.
(map below)

Drigg Railway

R. Mite

Ravenglass and Eskdale Railway

WHITEHAVEN

A.595

road

A.595

Castle car park

continuation on previous page

war memorial

farm

bus stop

railway stations

private road

public road

gate

gate

Ravenglass

tarn

gate

Roman Fort

Roman villa or bath house

this path
branches left
on grass from
the private road
just before a fork

R. ESK

R. ESK

191

Ponsonby Fell
1020'

950 feet of ascent

from GOSFORTH

7¼ miles
(+ 1½ on the bus)

4½ hours

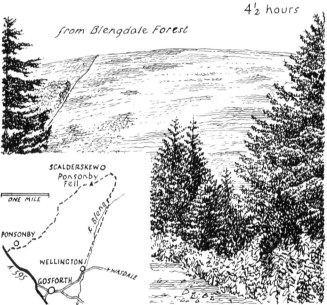

from Blengdale Forest

SCALDERSKEW ○
Ponsonby
Fell ▲

ONE MILE

PONSONBY ○

R. Blengd

WELLINGTON ↗ →WASDALE

A.595

GOSFORTH

There are no fells not worth climbing, but Ponsonby Fell is very nearly in this category.... The only justification for spending time on it is the splendid approach through Blengdale Forest, which, unlike most modern plantations, retains much of its natural deciduous woodlands and has many well-spaced mature conifers lining its riverside road.   Blengdale makes the climb worth while, but only just.

192

Leave Gosforth by the Wasdale road, which is fast
becoming built up with new dwellings, for a mile as far
as Wellington, where the quiet Blengdale road leaves
it to head directly up the valley of the Bleng alongside
the pleasant river. Beyond a cattle grid is the forest. A
simple bridge is crossed and the road forks. Take the
less obvious left branch and enter the finest section of
the forest with the river soon running close on the left.
Three-quarters of a mile further another fork occurs
in the road: branch left to the river, where progress is
halted at the abutments of a vanished bridge. 80 yards
upstream, however, is a footbridge. Use this to join the
forest road seen on the far bank: it curves uphill, and,
after being joined by another road on the right and one
on the left, heads straight for the open moor and leaves
the forest at a cattle grid with sheep pens adjacent. So
much for the forest. Now the road continues, curving
left to the isolated farm of Scalderskew, seen against a
backing of more plantations. Stockdale Moor, a site of
ancient settlements, is on the right. Go along the road
to a depression crossed by a wall and a stream. Here the
road continues up to Scalderskew over another cattle grid,
but preferably at this point cross the wall on the left at
a gate-cum-hurdle to gain access to the slopes of Ponsonby
Fell. There is a public path from the hurdle, not visible
and obviously never used, to a bridleway opposite the
farm, but waste no time looking for it and instead aim
for the top of the fell through a tangle of vegetation in
rich variety: heather, bracken and knee-height grass.
The ascent is slow and tedious, with only an overhead
cable by which to measure progress. The long grass
persists to the summit, which is duly attained with a
conviction that nobody has ever been there before: it
is surprising to find this impression contradicted by a
small heap of stones that some anonymous enthusiastic
cairn-builder has laboured to gather. Nor is the view
of Lakeland much reward, being severly restricted by
nearby Lank Rigg, Haycock and Seatallan.
   There is little cause to linger. Descend the seaward
side, west, to a gate in the wall on the left, the grass
here being waist-high. At the gate the bridleway from
Scalderskew is joined and progress is easier alongside
a wire fence, which cross at another gate and continue
in the same direction with the fence now on the right,
the way being pathless in an area of burnt gorse and
heather. The farm buildings of Laverock How appear in
sight ahead, amongst trees, and a clear track is joined
and followed down to the left where, beyond a gate, it
becomes a sunken lane between fences. Keep along this
to cross a ford near the farm of Scargreen and set foot
upon a not-unwelcome tarmac road, which is traffic free
and leads, as a leafy avenue framing the towers of the
atomic power station, to the A.595 at Ponsonby road-end,
where, if your timing is good, a bus will come along for
Gosforth in a few minutes. Be nice to sit down!

                    A map of the route is given overleaf →

MAP

The closing stages of this walk, on tarmac, are unsatisfactory, but a footpath that would give a direct route of return to Gosforth is fenced off and cannot be used despite the assurance given on the footpath map at the public car park at Gosforth that it is a right of way. In these circumstances the easiest course is as directed, i.e. to go down to the A.595 at Ponsonby and return to Gosforth by bus.
Or, if preferred, use the bus at the outset and reverse the route.

continuation at foot of next page ↓

rough road

River Bleng

STRANDS
WASDALE HEAD

Wellington Bridge

PONSONBY BUS STOP

A.595

300

200

Gosforth
car park

Church

road

SANTON BRIDGE

SEASCALE 2

HOLMROOK 2½

Don't plan to walk back along the A.595; it is busy, dangerous, and has no footpath.

continuation opposite

600

Laverock How (farm)

gate

500

lane

ONE MILE

two gates

500

ford

Scargreen (farm)

Ponsonby

500

road

400

PONSONBY OLD HALL

bus stop

A.595

CALDER BRIDGE 1¾

300

GOSFORTH 1½

in Blengdale Forest

194

MAP

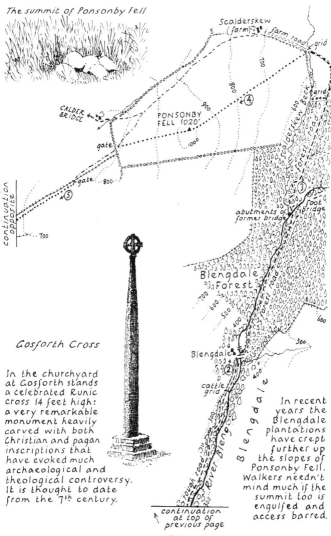

The summit of Ponsonby Fell

Scalderskew (farm)
farm road
grid

CALDER BRIDGE

PONSONBY FELL 1020

gate

800
900
1000

4

Scalderskew Beck

forest road

gate

800

5

continuation opposite

700

abutments of former bridge

foot bridge

3

Blengdale Forest

700
600
500
400

forest road

600

500

Blengdale

2

cattle grid

400

River Bleng

Blengdale

rough road

continuation at top of previous page

Gosforth Cross

In the churchyard at Gosforth stands a celebrated Runic cross 14 feet high: a very remarkable monument heavily carved with both Christian and pagan inscriptions that have evoked much archaeological and theological controversy. It is thought to date from the 7th century.

In recent years the Blengdale plantations have crept further up the slopes of Ponsonby Fell. Walkers needn't mind much if the summit too is engulfed and access barred.

Cold Fell
955'

260 feet of ascent

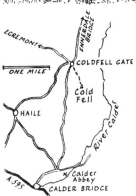

the summit

Cold Fell is an unremarkable
height, being merely a gentle
mile-long elevation overlooking
the lovely valley of the Calder,
but its name is well-known in
west Cumberland, having been
adopted for a popular high-level
road into Ennerdale leaving the
A.595 at Calder Bridge. The Coldfell Road, once a Roman
highway, forms the National Park boundary. Access to
the summit from this road is a very simple matter. The
ascent of Cold Fell may, however, be combined with a
visit to the most charming of Lakeland's packhorse
bridges, Matty Benn's Bridge (named 'Monks Bridge'
on Ordnance maps), the double objective providing an
outing both pleasant and non-arduous from a parked
car at Coldfell Gate.

196

ONE MILE

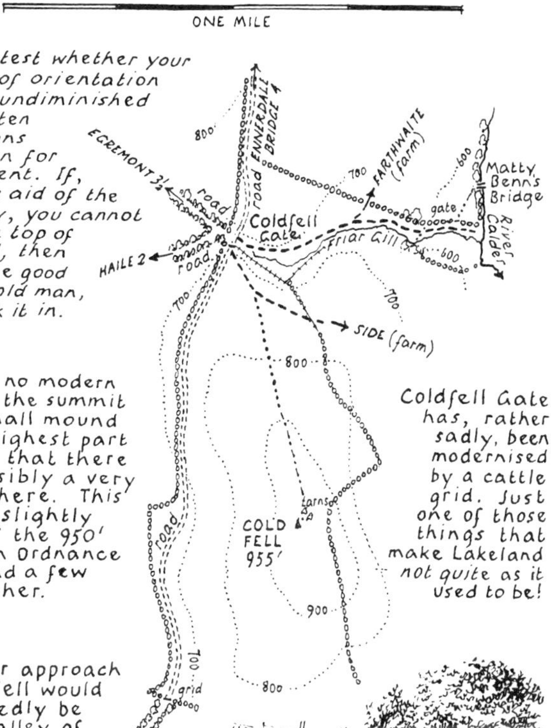

Just to test whether your powers of orientation remain undiminished no written directions are given for this ascent. If, with the aid of the map only, you cannot find the top of Cold Fell, then take some good advice, old man, and pack it in.

EGREMONT 3½
road
road ENNERDALE BRIDGE
FARTHWAITE (farm)
800'
700'
Matty Benn's Bridge
River Calder
gate
Coldfell Gate
Friar Gill
600'
HAILE 2
road
700'
SIDE (farm)
700'

There is no modern cairn on the summit but a small mound on the highest part suggests that there was possibly a very old one here. This point is slightly north of the 950' shown on Ordnance maps and a few feet higher.

800'

Coldfell Gate has, rather sadly, been modernised by a cattle grid. Just one of those things that make Lakeland not quite as it used to be!

road
700'
tarns
COLD FELL 955'
900'

A better approach to Cold Fell would undoubtedly be up the valley of the Calder from the romantic ruins of Calder Abbey, but public rights of way in this direction do not extend onto the fell.

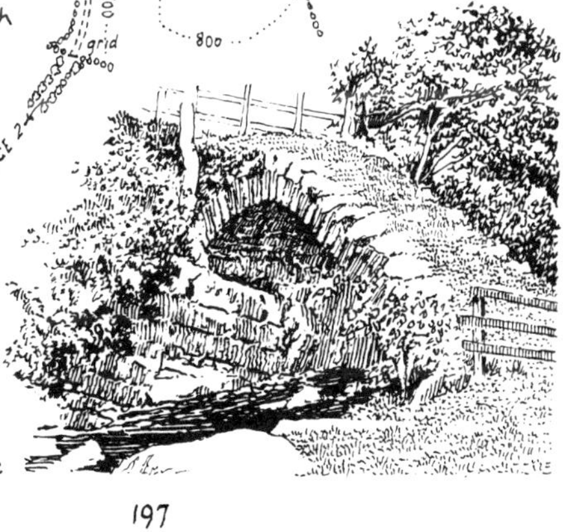

grid
CALDER BRIDGE 2
800'

Matty Benn's Bridge

Flat Fell and Dent
871'   1131'

1300 feet of ascent

Dent, from Flat Fell

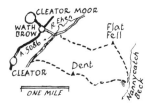

Wath Bridge

One does not expect to find open and unspoilt rural scenery only half an hour's stroll from an industrial environment, and the transition from the built-up plain of West Cumberland to the tranquil upland of Flat Fell is sudden and complete. This is a pleasant walk, enhanced by the charming oasis of Nannycatch. The neighbouring height, Dent, is not in the National Park but can conveniently be included in the walk.

The valley of
Nannycatch
Beck
as seen from
Flatfell Screes

Nannycatch
Gate and
Raven Crag

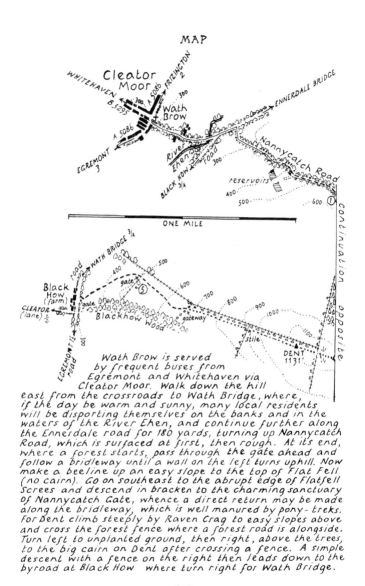

MAP

Cleator
Moor

Wath
Brow

ONE MILE

Wath Brow is served
by frequent buses from
Egremont and Whitehaven via
Cleator Moor. Walk down the hill
east from the crossroads to Wath Bridge, where,
if the day be warm and sunny, many local residents
will be disporting themselves on the banks and in the
waters of the River Ehen, and continue further along
the Ennerdale road for 180 yards, turning up Nannycatch
Road, which is surfaced at first, then rough. At its end,
where a forest starts, pass through the gate ahead and
follow a bridleway until a wall on the left turns uphill. Now
make a beeline up an easy slope to the top of Flat Fell
(no cairn). Go on southeast to the abrupt edge of Flatfell
Screes and descend in bracken to the charming sanctuary
of Nannycatch Gate, whence a direct return may be made
along the bridleway, which is well manured by pony-treks.
For Dent climb steeply by Raven Crag to easy slopes above
and cross the forest fence where a forest road is alongside.
Turn left to unplanted ground, then right, above the trees,
to the big cairn on Dent after crossing a fence. A simple
descent with a fence on the right then leads down to the
byroad at Black How where turn right for Wath Bridge.

200

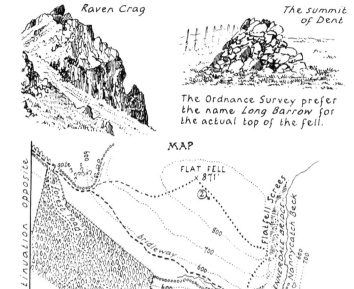

Raven Crag

The summit of Dent

The Ordnance Survey prefer the name *Long Barrow* for the actual top of the fell.

MAP

FLAT FELL
× 871'

continuation opposite

gate

Dent forest

bridleway

Flatfell Screes

ENNERDALE BRIDGE

Nannycatch Beck

Raven Crag

gate

Nannycatch Gate

KIRK BECK

EGREMONT

forest
water tank

The view from Dent

The green hill of Dent, once partly a deer park but now partly forest, is far superior to Flat Fell as a viewpoint. A wide panorama greets the eye. The whole of the Cumbrian coastal plain from Black Combe to the Solway Firth is in full view and crowded with detail. The seascape includes the Isle of Man, looking surprisingly near, and, distantly, the Galloway coast and, some say, Ireland. The view of the fells of Lakeland embraces the Loweswater heights (overtopped by Skiddaw and Grasmoor), the High Stile and Pillar groups enclosing Ennerdale, and, best of all, an exciting silhouette of Scafell Pike and Scafell. Of the lakes, only a section of Ennerdale Water is visible.

Dent has but a modest elevation, yet as a viewpoint it has great stature.

Watch Hill

visiting
   Watch Hill, 770'
   Setmurthy Common, 833'

600 feet of ascent

from the A.66

4 miles

2 hours

The main road into Cockermouth from the east passes for several miles in the lee of a long low ridge partly under forest and not having much visual appeal. The western part, however, gives a splendid traverse of open upland and fine views. It is easily attained with a minimum of effort: a stroll on grass so simple that boots are incongruous footwear for it and bare feet appropriate.

below:
   the summit of Watch Hill
right:
   the summit at 833'

202

MAP

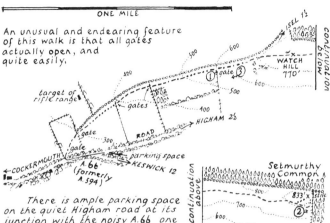

ONE MILE

An unusual and endearing feature of this walk is that all gates actually open, and quite easily.

target of rifle range

gates

gate

gate

ROAD

parking space

←COCKERMOUTH

A.66 (formerly A.594)

KESWICK 12

HIGHAM 2½

WATCH HILL 770'

ISEL 1½

continuation below

continuation above

Setmurthy Common

833' stile

   There is ample parking space on the quiet Higham road at its junction with the noisy A.66 one mile out of Cockermouth. Walk towards the town for 200 yards to a public footpath sign at a gate, which enter and cross the field diagonally to another gate (note a benchmark on the gatepost). A wall starts here and is kept on the left as the path, intermittent in places, ascends gently through a succession of kissing gates. When the wall turns away left continue forward up a wide green strip to the top of the rise. This is Watch Hill; no cairn. A most delightful promenade on turf close-cropped by sheep along an undulating ridge with a plantation on the left, then follows until another plantation is met across the line of march. The highest point of the fell occurs in the corner formed by the forest; no cairn. A step-stile here admits to a break in the trees: an alternative route of return would be by forest road descending to the Higham road a mile and a half from the car, but it is infinitely more pleasurable to reverse the route of ascent and so enjoy a second time the excellent panorama from Watch Hill.

Watch Hill is well named. It commands a splendid view of the Cockermouth district, but fellwalkers will prefer to survey the array of mountains seen southwards, the principal ones being, left to right:

The Skiddaw group
Sale Fell
Great Dodd
Watson's Dodd
Lord's Seat
Grisedale Pike
Hopegill Head
Grasmoor
Whiteside
High Stile
Red Pike
Scoat Fell
Haycock
Mellbreak
Starling Dodd
Great Borne
Fellbarrow
The Loweswater Fells.

Clints Crags

804'

300 feet of ascent

from BLINDCRAKE

3 miles

1½ hours

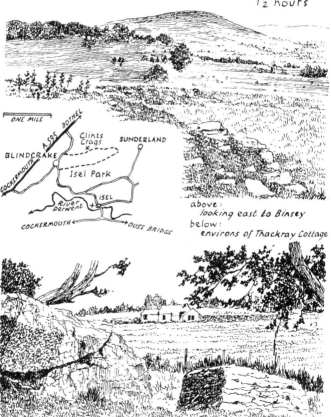

ONE MILE

BOTHEL

A.595

Clints
Crags
×

BLINDCRAKE

SUNDERLAND

COCKERMOUTH

Isel Park

River
Derwent

ISEL

COCKERMOUTH ←

→ OUSE BRIDGE

above:
looking east to Binsey
below:
environs of Thackray Cottage

MAP

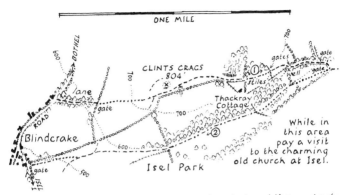

ONE MILE

BOTHEL

CLINTS CRAGS
.804.

lane

ROAD

Blindcrake

Thackray
Cottage

While in
this area
pay a visit
to the charming
old church at Isel.

Isel Park

This is a walk on public footpaths, but until somebody removes the barbed wire and other obstacles to legitimate progress it can be recommended only to gymnasts.

Assuming the right of unimpeded passage is restored (a protest is needed) leave the north end of Blindcrake hamlet by a lane going east. This promises well but soon becomes choked by shoulder-high vegetation, desperate struggling being necessary to reach a gate (viciously barricaded at the time of writing) that gives, or should, access to open fell. A simple, five-minute ascent leads to the highest point of Clints Crags, which has been quarried. Below it, a good path continues forward to a limestone escarpment to end at a barbed stile. If this can be negotiated, contour alongside a wood, climbing gates to reach Willie White's Well, amongst trees in a hollow on the right. Here a gated lane is joined.

Go along it, no longer expecting gates to open, and around a corner on the right, at another gate, double back on an invisible footpath between plantations in pleasant parkland with fewer obstacles to join a wall and so emerge on the road opposite the inn at Blindcrake. The last gate actually opens.

Limestone escarpment
near Thackray Cottage

The best features of the view from Clints Crag are southeast and south: to the deep basin of Bassenthwaite Lake and the skyline of the Lorton and Crummock mountains.

Caermote Hill

920'
(not named on 1" Ordnance maps)

500 feet of ascent

from BOTHEL

4½ miles

2½ hours

from the
Roman Fort

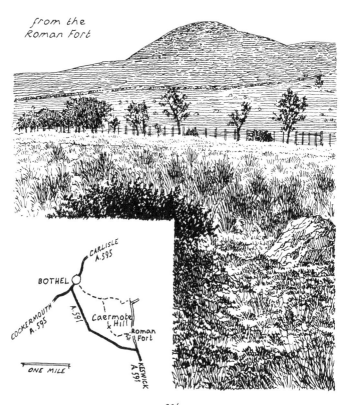

There is little visually attractive about Caermote Hill, which appears as a bare mound above gentle slopes descending to the Keswick-Carlisle road A.591, but it has a significant place in local history and the cattle and sheep that now graze in undisturbed tranquillity do in fact tread ground that once was in more active occupation. An ancient earthwork on the top, circular in plan, is of obscure purpose and origin, nearby is an "official" beacon site used when communications were primitive, while at the foot of the hill are distinct traces of a little-known Roman Fort. Today there is an air of neglect about these mute reminders of past civilisations although the Fort has been the subject of recent attention.

The Roman Fort

The site of the fort is just sufficiently elevated to command a view down the Bassenthwaite valley, but its position appears to have been selected for other than strategic reasons, particularly as it occurs well away from the main Roman highway connecting the forts of Papcastle and Old Carlisle; possibly it was a depot. Sections have been excavated, sufficient to establish that there were two forts, a large one of rectangular outline with rounded corners and a small one abutting. The ground is swampy and the existence of a hard road to give dry access has been discovered on the east side (now cut through by the modern road alongside). The walls of the fort were of turf reinforced by stones and the outer parapet is still easily identifiable.

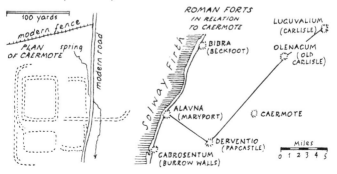

The memorial boulder,
Caermote Hill

Two plaques, each a memorial to a local man whose ashes
were scattered at this spot, are affixed to the sides of the
boulder and inscribed:

WALTER S DEAN   JACK ROUTLEDGE
1890-1967   1905-1965

That they are still in pristine condition is an emphasis
on the remoteness of this fell and infrequency of visitors.

The summit of
Caermote Hill

Binsey in the
background

MAP

ONE MILE

Bothel · school
layby parking

The village of Bothel stands at
a junction of main roads — the
A.595 (Cockermouth - Carlisle) and
the A.591 (Keswick - Carlisle), both
with bus services.

④

①

③

site of
beacon

earthwork

St. John's
Hill

gate

old
mine

CAERMOTE
HILL
920'

ROAD

②

gate

gate

Caermote
Roman Fort

A lane turns off the A.595 at
Beck House, fords a stream (a
slab footbridge is provided for
pedestrians) and leads pleasantly
to two facing gates. Take the one
on the right (muddy) and continue
forward, ascending gently, using
two more gates, with an arable
field between and a fence on the
right, to reach the ridge ahead in
a jungle of gorse. Here the fence is
succeeded by a broken wall, which
cross at a gap, leaving the public
footpath, and turn south alongside
the ridge-fence. Progress is halted
when a barbed fence crosses the line
of march: evidence that there is no
right of way. Negotiate this obstacle
with difficulty. There is now a wall on
the left; over it, on the brow of the hill,
can be seen the outlines of an earthwork,
obviously ancient. The flat summit mound
is the site of a beacon. Continue south, doing
nothing to annoy the grazing cows in case one is a bull, and, from
a gate in the wall-corner ahead, attain the more-fell-like top of
Caermote Hill, which has a few embedded boulders (one having
two plaques) and a lovely view of Bassenthwaite Lake. A steep
descent (beware rabbit-holes) now leads to a gate in a corner,
through (or over) which turn left by a fence to reach a tarmac
side-road at a gate after inspecting the remains of Caermote
Roman Fort. Turn left along the road for two-thirds of a mile
until it turns sharp right, when go forward up the rough lane
facing. From this, two side-lanes turn off left (see map). The
first offers a quick way back to the ridge-fence but involves
the unlawful crossing of two fields; the second is a long way
round but is more likely to have the farmer's blessing. From
the ridge return to Bothel by the outward route.

Faulds Brow
1125'
600 feet of ascent

ONE MILE

WIGTON

B.5299

→ CARLISLE

Faulds
Brow

WHELPO

CALDBECK

B.5299

← KESWICK

Carrock Fell and High Pike,
from Faulds Brow

Faulds Brow is the most northerly of the outlying fells within the National Park. It is unremarkable in appearance, being merely a slight upland dome alongside the Keswick-Carlisle unenclosed by-road above Caldbeck, but its easy slopes are sufficiently elevated to give an uninterrupted view across the wide coastal plain to the Solway Firth, backed by the Scottish hills with Criffell prominent, while to the south the Skiddaw massif forms a near horizon and Lakeland's western fells appear more distantly to its right. Very conspicuous in the scene are two television masts: a BBC mast on Sandale Fell, west, and an ITV mast at Waverhead, due north. Faulds Brow is clothed in short heather, affording pleasant walking uninterrupted by walls or fences along an easy ridge accessible from the by-road, where cars may be parked on the verges at several places and the summit reached in ten minutes, but, to make a worthwhile walk, the ascent is described from the village of Caldbeck.

Shooting butt on Faulds Brow

Crater on Faulds Brow; ITV mast in background

211

ONE MILE

This wall, marking a parish boundary, has been adopted as the National Park boundary also.

craters

FAULDS BROW 1125'

shooting butts

old quarry

ROAD

continuation opposite

pastures

shakeholes

ROAD

KESWICK 14

900

800

700

800

700

Whelpo Beck

Whelpo

KESWICK 14

This is a walk mostly on motor roads, but they are pleasant and quiet. You are not likely to get knocked down.

Leave Caldbeck by the Wigton and Carlisle road but preferably deviate in the first section by going round to it by way of the old mill and the village green: a pleasing detour. Then proceed up the road until a lane branches off to the left, and follow this to emerge on an unenclosed fell road (Keswick-Carlisle) opposite the access to Waverhead Farm. Cross the road and bear left onto moorland, where easy walking in short heather leads to a series of small craters, not natural shakeholes but suggesting that a stick of bombs was jettisoned here. Beyond is an old quarry and then the gentle summit of Faulds Brow, a lovely carpet of heather contaminated and disgraced by the presence of four shooting butts erected by brave British sportsmen. A slight subsidiary rise to the south has a cairn of sorts and overlooks the fell road: note the junction with the Whelpo byroad, half-right, and aim for it (some shakeholes hereabouts). Go down to Whelpo on the tarmac or its wide grass margins, crossing a bridge over Whelpo Beck (notable for its rampant mimulus) at the foot of the hill, and joining another road, which, followed left, leads back to Caldbeck.

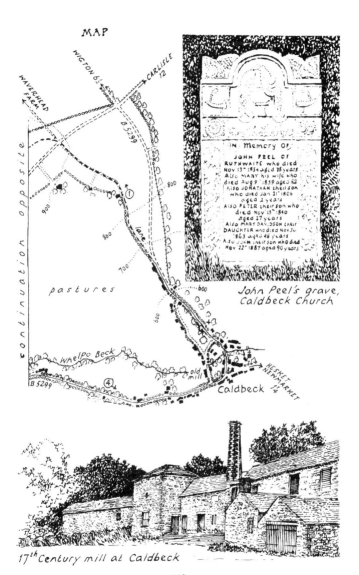

MAP

WAVERHEAD FARM

WIGTON 6½

CARLISLE 12

B 5299

900

800

800

800

700

lane

①

pastures

continuation opposite

600

600

Whelpo Beck

old mill

④

B 5299

Caldbeck

HESKET NEWMARKET 1¼

IN Memory of

JOHN PEEL OF
RUTHWAITE who died
NOV 13th 1854 aged 78 years
ALSO MARY his wife who
died Aug 9 1859 aged 82
ALSO JONATHAN their son
who died Jan 21st 1806
aged 2 years
ALSO PETER their son who
died Nov 13th 1840
aged 27 years
ALSO MARY DAVIDSON their
DAUGHTER who died Nov 30
1863 aged 48 years
ALSO JOHN their son who died
Nov 22nd 1887 aged 90 years

John Peel's grave,
Caldbeck Church

17th Century mill at Caldbeck

213

Dunmallet
775'

(not named on 1" Ordnance maps;
named "Dunmallard Hill"
on 2½" Ordnance maps)

300 feet of ascent

from POOLEY BRIDGE

1 mile
there and back

1 hour

*Dunmallet,
from Pooley Bridge*

Dunmallet is the prominent hill at the
foot of Ullswater, wooded from tip to
toe and looking not at all suitable for
a fellwalking expedition.   Nor is it,
the only attraction being a pleasant
woodland path and, for a learned few,
the remains (barely distinguishable) of
a fort that probably dates from early
Celtic times when the hill was a bare
rocky mound and is thought to have been
abandoned when Dacre Castle was built.

214

MAP

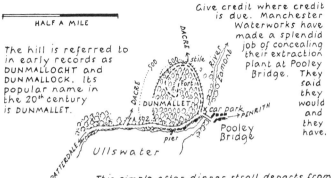

HALF A MILE

The hill is referred to in early records as DUNMALLOGHT and DUNMALLOCK. Its popular name in the 20th century is DUNMALLET.

Give credit where credit is due. Manchester Waterworks have made a splendid job of concealing their extraction plant at Pooley Bridge. They said they would and they have.

DACRE · 500 · stile · River Eamont · Fort · DUNMALLET · DACRE · car park · PENRITH · Pooley Bridge · pier · ? · PATTERDALE · Ullswater

This simple after-dinner stroll departs from the Cumberland (west) side of Pooley Bridge by the footpath signposted 'Dacre' near the car park, and climbs in a spiral around steep wooded slopes to arrive at the top of Dunmallet from the south. The path is distinct throughout and continues from the top to cross the scanty remains of the earthworks of the fort and slope down to rejoin the outward route opposite a stile indicating the way to Dacre.

There is nothing to mark the summit. It was formerly a triangulation station but is now buried in undergrowth of tropical prodigality, mainly blackberries, below a canopy of foliage. For this reason there is no distant view. It used to be said of Dunmallet that it overlooked Ullswater. Today you cannot see the lake for the trees.

Dunmallet, from Ullswater

215

Heughscar Hill
1231'
750 feet of ascent

from the
Stone Circle

The Romans knew Heughscar Hill, though not by that name, and laid their High Street along its western flank. Today, pony-trekkers enjoy this historic highway.

Heughscar Hill is the gentlest of eminences. It is easily reached by a stroll from Westmorland's most attractive village, Askham, and commands a fine prospect, including a lovely view of Ullswater with the lofty Helvellyn range forming a majestic background. It is clothed in patches of bracken and a velvet turf on which carpet slippers would be more appropriate than boots, but its greatest joy is the spine of limestone outcropping in rocky pavements along the top.

The hill overlooks a rough plateau, Moor Divock, the site of many antiquities, suggesting that long before the Romans came the ancient Britons had already found the place to their liking.

So will modern Britons, especially those hovering on the verge of becoming ancient. Heughscar Hill is a gem for aged fellwalkers.

Ullswater, from the summit

MAP

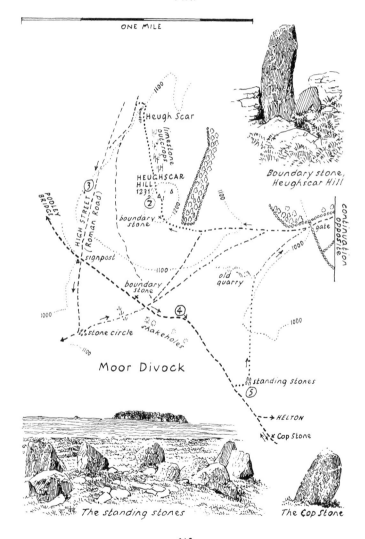

ONE MILE

Heugh Scar

limestone outcrops

HEUGHSCAR HILL 1291

② boundary stone

③

POOLEY BRIDGE

HIGH STREET (Roman Road)

signpost

Boundary stone, Heughscar Hill

gate

continuation opposite

1000

1100

1000

boundary stone

old quarry

④

shakeholes

stone circle

1000

1100

Moor Divock

standing stones

⑤

→ HELTON

✗ Cop Stone

The standing stones

The Cop Stone

Depart from Askham, a charming village,
by the rising street to the west, which ends
at a cattle grid. A good path goes ahead with
a wall on the right. Ignore a tarmac strip and
later a gravel road both branching left, keeping
uphill, now on grass, to a gate giving access to open fell.
Indefinite tracks lead forward: take the one up a gentle
incline to the right, on lovely turf, aiming for the corner
of a plantation half a mile ahead. Just before reaching it
a clearer path turns off downhill, but ignore this and go
along the side of the plantation to a prominent inscribed
boundary stone, beyond which is the cairn indicating the
top of Heughscar Hill, where a lovely view of Ullswater is
seen backed by Helvellyn; to the east the Cross Fell range
stands up well. Patches of bracken, green turf and natural
rock gardens of limestone make this a delectable place on
a sunny day.

Continue north along the top, with a line of outcropping
rock on the right, and over the limestone crag (Heugh Scar)
seen in profile ahead, descending beyond it in bracken to
join a clear path running below it. Follow this to the left.
Diversions created by pony-trekkers have in places obscured
the original course of the path (the Roman High Street): a
line taken west of south will, however, reach a wide green
track (Pooley Bridge - Helton) at a cairn and signpost. Go
across this, continuing south on the High Street, to a stone
circle, from which cut across to the green track and follow
it south-east as far as the Cop Stone, prominently seen on
the skyline. Now retrace steps for a quarter-mile and then
turn onto the moor on the right to find, in 100 yards, a tidy
cluster of standing stones. All these relics are of great age.
Being an antiquity yourself, it boosts morale exceedingly to
find things even older than you are. With an inspired new
buoyancy of stride (but, please, no singing) scamper across
the moor north to the scanty remains of a quarry, where a
simple traverse north-east leads back to the fell gate.

Return thence to Askham by the outward route.

Knipescar Common

1118'

from SCARSIDE

300 feet of ascent

3½ miles

2 hours

The band of limestone along the eastern fringe of Lakeland influences the landscape at several places and is immediately recognisable on sight. Such a place is Knipe Scar, a lofty escarpment bordering the Lowther Castle parkland estates and overlooking the valley of the River Lowther. The Scar itself consists of no more than minor outcrops on a horizontal plane but the flat top

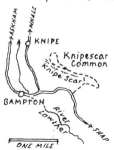

is a green sward interlaced in parts by weathered limestone, with, unexpectedly, a scattering of 'foreign' boulders left there by a retreating glacier. Knipe Scar is virtually unknown, away from beaten tracks and rarely visited, but ancient remains indicate that it once housed a primitive human settlement.

The mile-long green terrace along the rim of the Scar is a most delightful ramble.

limestone pavement

looking southwest from the summit

SELSIDE PIKE   BRANSTREE   HARTER FELL   ILL BELL   MARDALE ILL BELL   HIGH STREET

Naddle Forest   Mardale

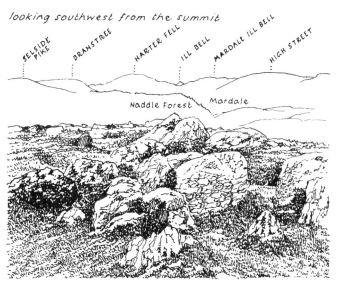

The ancient enclosure, indicated on some maps as a Stone Circle and formerly referred to locally as a Druids Circle, is a sad disappointment visually, and would be difficult to locate were it not for a Ministry of Works sign proclaiming it a protected ancient monument; even with this help the 'circle' is not obvious amongst the natural litter of boulders and bracken. Unlike other such monuments the stones have not been brought to the site but are naturally embedded and added to by others cleared to leave a circle of open ground except for one large boulder retained in the middle. In the adjoining plantation, now inaccessible, are the earthworks of a settlement.

above
old limekiln

left
erratic boulder
on a limestone plinth

MAP

ONE MILE

Not the least of the attractions
of Knipe Scar is its far-reaching
views. Although the High Street
range conceals most of Lakeland
to the west, Blencathra is an
impressive sight. Eastwards
there is a continuous skyline
of the higher Pennines
from Cross Fell south
to the Mallerstang
and Howgill Fells.

(1000)
ancient
enclosure
KNIPESCAR
COMMON
Scarside
Plantation
Knipe
Scar
Inscar
Plantation
gate
gorse
Scar
Plantation
1000
BAMPTON
900
gate
Scarside
(farm)
lime
kiln
gate
900

The simplest way
onto Knipescar Common
is by the lane (a right of
way) past Scarside Farm,
leaving a corner on the
Shap-Bampton
road with the
advantage of a
start at 850'. There
is limited parking on
the roadside nearby.
  The lane is surfaced to
the farm and continues
beyond as a grass track
between walls to a gate at
the end. From this point
there is unimpeded walking
on the Common. Limestone

SHAP 2½

Haweswater is best seen
from the southeast end
of the Common.

and sheep, in combination, provide the best surface for
walking known to man, and so it is here.   Ascend to a
gate ahead in the plantation wall (a well-built structure
of dry limestone). Do not pass through the gate (which in
faded lettering carries a message about a bull) but turn
left alongside the wall on a pleasant cart track fringed
by a forest of gorse. Further, in open ground, the track
swings away from the wall along a green terrace (once a
race-track for the local sports) between the headland of
the scar on the left and limestone outcrops on the right.
When the track curves to the right and starts to descend
gently amongst bracken leave it and, aiming for the wall,
go in search of an ancient enclosure marked by a sign. A
return to the 'bull' gate can then be made by traversing
the top of the Common (summit indefinite; note many
erratic boulders) and regaining the path.   More of this
delightful promenade can be enjoyed by continuing from
the gate to the south-east end of the Common, returning
at a lower level past a lime kiln to the Scarside gate and
so back to the car.

The Naddle Horseshoe

visiting

Scalebarrow Knott, 1109'
Harper Hills, 1358'
Hare Shaw, 1639'
Nameless summits, 1427', 1380'
   and 1320', in Naddle Forest
Hugh's Laithes Pike, 1390'

from SWINDALE

8 miles

5 hours

1450 feet of ascent

This is not the caravan-infested Naddle between
Keswick and Thirlmere. It is the caravan-free
Naddle near the Haweswater dam.

The Naddle valley, from Hare Shaw

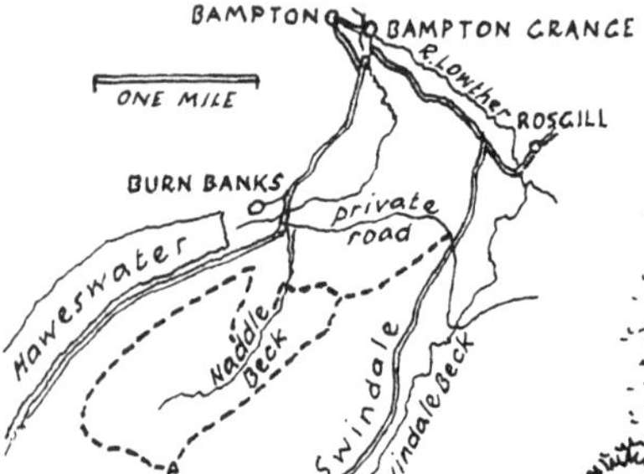

Mardale, once a walkers' valley, has become a motorists' way to the hills and an increasing number of cars speed along the road provided by Manchester Corporation on the east side of Haweswater and use the parking places at the head of the reservoir. In so doing they pass the entrance to a small side-valley of attractive appearance, being inurned between steep and craggy slopes draped with mature woodland, a natural forest centuries old; but, having no public road along which cars may be taken, it rarely gets more than a passing glance from visitors on wheels. This valley is the Naddle, a typical Lakeland backwater that has happily escaped 'development' by the two great predators — the Forestry Commission and M.C.W.W. (initials that need no translation), and although the latter authority's Swindale aqueduct briefly emerges above ground as it crosses Naddle Beck, to their credit they have concealed its presence well. It is a quiet valley with one farm only and beyond its enclosing arms an undulating plateau of rough pasture with a fine view of the mountains around Mardale that few walkers ever come to see.

Reservoir, Harper Hills
(on the Swindale supply line)

The walk described starts on Rosgill Moor at the foot of the next valley, Swindale; follows Naddle's eastern ridge (Swindale Common), crosses the plateau to reach the western ridge (Naddle Forest) and descends into the Naddle valley to return to the starting point.

225

Summit cairn,
Scalebarrow Knott

Summit rocks,
Hare Shaw

This is the first summit of Hare Shaw reached on the walk.
The next undulation west is the highest point of the fell —
it has traces of a former triangulation station.

The ridge of Naddle Forest,
from point 1380'

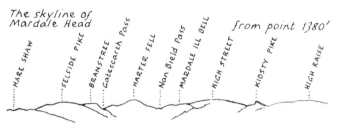

The skyline of
Mardale Head   from point 1380'

HARE SHAW · SELSIDE PIKE · BRANSTREE · Gatescarth Pass · HARTER FELL · Nan Bield Pass · MARDALE ILL BELL · HIGH STREET · KIDSTY PIKE · HIGH RAISE

Hugh's Laithes Pike,
looking down to
Haweswater dam.

MAP

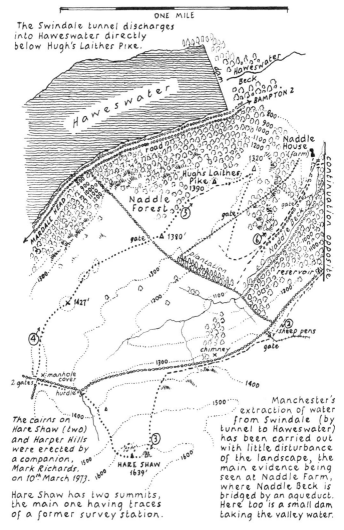

ONE MILE

The Swindale tunnel discharges
into Haweswater directly
below Hugh's Laithes Pike.

Haweswater

Haweswater Beck

BAMPTON 2

800
900
1000
1100
1200

Naddle House (farm)

1320

③

Hugh's Laithes Pike ▲ 1390

Naddle Forest

MARDALE HEAD

800
900
1000
1200

road

gate

gate

⑥ Naddle Beck

continuation opposite

▲ 1380'

Plantation

reservoir

1100

1200

1300

1300

× 1427'

1200

1200

④

② sheep pens

gate

chimney
×

1300

1400

× manhole cover

2 gates

hurdle

1400

1500

③

HARE SHAW 1639'

1600

The cairns on
Hare Shaw (two)
and Harper Hills
were erected by
a companion,
Mark Richards,
on 10ᵗʰ March 1973.

Hare Shaw has two summits,
the main one having traces
of a former survey station.

Manchester's
extraction of water
from Swindale (by
tunnel to Haweswater)
has been carried out
with little disturbance
of the landscape, the
main evidence being
seen at Naddle Farm,
where Naddle Beck is
bridged by an aqueduct.
Here too is a small dam
taking the valley water.

MAP

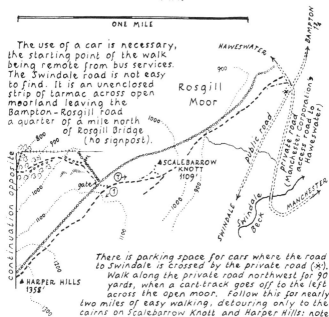

ONE MILE

The use of a car is necessary, the starting point of the walk being remote from bus services. The Swindale road is not easy to find. It is an unenclosed strip of tarmac across open moorland leaving the Bampton-Rosgill road a quarter of a mile north of Rosgill Bridge (no signpost).

HAWESWATER

BAMPTON 1½

Rosgill Moor

public road

private road (Manchester Corporation access road to Haweswater)

▲ SCALEBARROW KNOTT 1109'

SWINDALE

Swindale Beck

MANCHESTER

continuation opposite

▲ HARPER HILLS 1358'

There is parking space for cars where the road to Swindale is crossed by the private road (✕). Walk along the private road northwest for 90 yards, when a cart-track goes off to the left across the open moor. Follow this for nearly two miles of easy walking, detouring only to the cairns on Scalebarrow Knott and Harper Hills: note the reservoir near the latter. Go on by the wall, descending to cross a gated fence and climbing again to pass a chimney-stack (surviving relic of a building, over the wall) and after a further quarter-mile leave the wall and aim south over rising ground to Hare Shaw. Then descend to rejoin the wall, now seen crossing a depression northwest. Pass a hurdle at a bend in the wall, keeping on the south side to the ridge ahead, where a fine view of the Mardale mountains is revealed. Two gates give access to the heathery continuation of the ridge northeast. A gate in a crosswall a mile forward admits to the final section of the ridge, which has three cairned summits, the second having an aerial view of the Haweswater dam. From the third a beeline to the Naddle valley is impracticable because of crags and trees. Instead, aim west of south to a gate in a fence and continue in the same direction to join a cart-track that loops down into the valley, which is then followed down, in natural woodlands, to Naddle Farm. Just short of the farm buildings, go through a wide gate on the right to ford the stream bed between a dam and an aqueduct bridge. Go up to a facing gate and follow an old bridleway (not clear at first, but becoming so) that slants uphill half-left by a tumbled wall to a gate in the ridgewall, whence the outward route is reversed for an easy mile to the car.

Howes

visiting
Nabs Moor, 1613'
Howes, 1930'

from SWINDALE HEAD

5¼ miles

3 hours

1100 feet of ascent

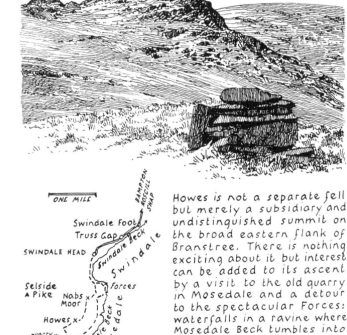

ONE MILE

Howes is not a separate fell but merely a subsidiary and undistinguished summit on the broad eastern flank of Branstree. There is nothing exciting about it but interest can be added to its ascent by a visit to the old quarry in Mosedale and a detour to the spectacular Forces: waterfalls in a ravine where Mosedale Beck tumbles into the strange upper recesses of Swindale Head.

Mosedale
Cottage

This walk is included only with some reservations for car-borne walkers. The valley road to Swindale Head is public but single-track and adequate only for local farm traffic. Above Truss Gap although tarmac-surfaced it narrows to axle-width without verges or passing places and a confrontation of cars or a meeting with straying sheep could cause delay and trouble and possibly even bad language.

Cars may be taken through to Swindale Head and left at the farm, and this is often done, but it is a courtesy to local users of the road to park in a layby at the end of the open moor section where it becomes enclosed near Swindale Foot; or at least take the car no further than Truss Gap. This means extra walking, but the flowery hedges, utter tranquillity and loveliness all around, not appreciated in a car, are recompense enough. An even better idea is to visit Swindale by bicycle.

This is one of many Lakeland daleheads from which pleasure-motorists should be excluded. Improving and widening the roads is most definitely NOT a solution. Swindale is unspoilt. Let's leave it that way.

Nabs Crag and
Dod Bottom

The Forces
below: *the top waterfall*
opposite: *the ravine*

The walk proper starts at Swindale Head Farm and miles are measured from there. Go up the valley (slightly down, actually) through a succession of gates along an unkempt walled lane, passing the ruins of High Swindale Head, to a gate at its end. The scene ahead is impressive. A thin path goes forward across a home-made bridge to an area of fine drumlins, winding in and out and over them with a swamp (an old tarn bed) on the right and Nab Crags in front bounded by a fearful gully. In an enclosed field on the left is Simon Stone, a large boulder in a copse of trees. Beyond the drumlins the path (a bridleway) ascends the fellside, becoming less distinct. Upon reaching a beck follow it upstream into an obvious breach in Nab Crags, so gaining the grassy top of Nabs Moor. Aim south from here to straddle a wire fence (which, to the right, is seen going up to the top of Selside Pike) and continue to an outcrop of rocks, where there is a cairn (the only one seen all day). Swing to the right now to the indefinite summit of Howes, passing an unexpected tarn. Mosedale Cottage is now in view. Contour forward to cross a streamlet (the slope ahead rises to Branstree), then slant easily downhill to cross a fence and descend to the Mosedale cart-track. (If desired, an interesting hour may be spent exploring the huge quarry nearby; Mosedale Cottage, a lonely outpost, is used by shepherds). Follow the cart-track left through desolation profound — deer may be noticed here — but when it turns towards a wooden bridge across the beck leave it and keep on forward, inclining left to avoid wet ground and coming alongside a broken wall, where a former bridleway, long out of favour, appears as a thin rut in the grass. Follow the wall north, passing a good sheepfold and another not so good. The Selside fence is again crossed, this time at a gate; soon after, the wall veers away on the right. Keeping forward, a perched boulder is reached and a view of Swindale opens ahead. The bridleway vanishes underfoot here, but never mind, for at this point you aim across rough ground to the right to enjoy the highlight of the walk: the Swindale waterfalls (marked 'Forces on 1" Ordnance maps). Here the beck tumbles down a rough and rocky ravine in a series of waterfalls and cascades, well viewed (with care) from the west bank, which is descended amongst outcrops to the valley floor. The scenery of this wild cleft is extremely fine, up to Lodore standard. Here is an unknown corner of Lakeland that would be ruined by countless picnickers if it were more easily accessible. So keep it under your hat. Go downstream to rejoin the path over the drumlins, returning along the lane to Swindale Head. If your bike has vanished, which is unlikely, you should have thought to pin a note to it saying you would be back to collect it.

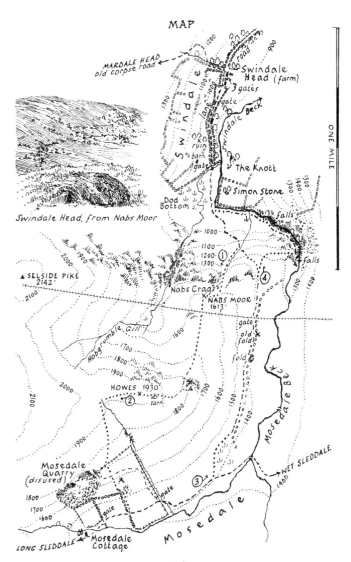

Seat Robert

visiting

Langhowe Pike, 1313'
Great Ladstones, 1439'
Seat Robert, 1688'
High Wether Howe, 1705'
Fewling Stones, 1667'

1100 feet of ascent

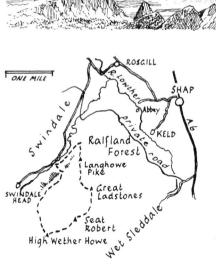

Seat Robert,
from
High Wether Howe

Swindale was threatened with a reservoir, but has escaped with an unobtrusive intake works and an unseen tunnel. Here Manchester has adopted methods of water extraction that are wholly to be commended.

Seat Robert is one of those out-of-the-way summits that all addicted fellwalkers notice from time to time in their study of the maps of Lakeland and vow to visit someday. But few do. It is too remote from the attractive interior of the district, and obviously nothing exciting is likely to be found in the grassy upland wilderness of Ralfland Forest out of which it rises to form the culminating point. This is the area of high ground lying between Swindale and Wet Sleddale and sloping gently to the valley of the River Lowther at Shap Abbey — a vast sheep pasture traversed by an ancient corpse road, an old bridleway and a network of tracks made by sheep (the first fellwalkers of all) and not by human pedestrians. The cairns on the highest tops are the work of shepherds and serve as guides, recognisable landmarks in mist and storm. This is confusing country.

The round of the summits described in this chapter is, however, a worthwhile expedition on a clear day, not so much for the views, which are extensive but dreary and uninspiring, as for the exhilaration of new territory, solace of solitude, and beneficial exercise.

Seat Robert provides these rewards.

Gowther Crag

top left: *cairn on Langhowe Pike*

top right: *cairn on Rowantree Crag*

right: *Rowantree Crag*

bottom left:
   cairn on
   Great Ladstones

bottom right:
   cairn on
   Gambling Crag

Ordnance
Survey 'ring'
embedded here

above:
  summit of Seat Robert

right:
  Beastman's Crag

below:
  Gouther Crag,
  from the
  footbridge.

There is limited space for roadside car parking 60 yards before reaching the footbridge over Swindale Beck near Truss Gap.

Cross the footbridge and a tract of rough ground to join an excellent path, which follow to the left, rising steadily for a full mile across a colourful fellside of bracken and gorse and boulders topped by a line of crags. When the skyline is reached and stone walls appear ahead, take a path branching sharp right (50 yards short of a fenced enclosure that formerly contained a rain gauge) and so reach the indefinite ridge above, where aim south for the cairn on Langhowe Pike. Here the next section of the route can be surveyed: the cairns on Great Ladstones and Gambling Crag are seen on the skyline to the left of the shallow pyramid of Seat Robert, below which, in a depression, is the dark tor of Rowantree Crag, the next objective, reached over easy ground avoiding marshes. After a fruitless search for a rowan tree, aim next for Great Ladstones, crossing a stream. The view now widens to include the long intake wall of Wet Sleddale. Go on south to the prominent cairn above Gambling Crag, then across a depression and a sheep-bridge to the summit of Seat Robert, which is capped with a heap of stones like a tumulus and has an Ordnance Survey 'ring' embedded in the ground. Haskew Tarn is now in sight with the return ridge beyond. Make for High Wether Howe, with a fence now on the left. Then descend by the broad ridge to the north, over Fewling Stones. Down to the left is seen the impressive head of Swindale backed by Selside Pike and Branstree. A cart-track runs below the splintered rocks of Beastman's Crag and continues to Haskew Beck, where go downstream to the corner of the substantial wall that keeps sheep away from the dangerous Gouther Crag. Here cross the stream above a wooded ravine, which, backed by the crag, makes an exciting picture, and swing round in a wide loop to the right to join a path that descends pleasantly through bracken to the footbridge and the car.

A feature of the walk is the complete absence of walls and fences across the route described: all of it is free and open walking — no gates and no stiles. A few wet patches make this a walk to be done only in dry weather, never in rain, and, being pathless, on the tops, certainly never in mist.

footbridge, Swindale Beck

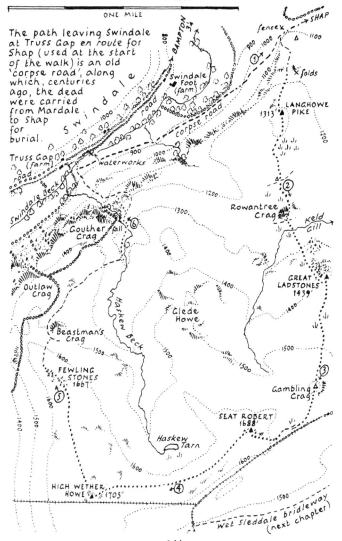

ONE MILE

The path leaving Swindale at Truss Gap en route for Shap (used at the start of the walk) is an old 'corpse road', along which, centuries ago, the dead were carried from Mardale to Shap for burial.

BAMPTON 3½

SHAP

fence

folds

Swindale Foot (farm)

Swindale

corpse road

LANGHOWE PIKE
1313

Truss Gap (farm)

waterworks

Swindale Beck

road

Rowantree Crag

Keld Gill

Gouther Crag

Outlaw Crag

Haskew Beck

Clede Howe

GREAT LADSTONES
1439

Beastman's Crag

FEWLING STONES
1667

SEAT ROBERT
1638

Gambling Crag

Haskew Tarn

HIGH WETHER HOWE
1705

Wet Sleddale bridleway (next chapter)

The Wet Sleddale Horseshoe

visiting
Sleddale Pike, 1659'
Great Saddle Crag, 1850'
Ulthwaite Rigg, 1648'

from the
RESERVOIR DAM

9¾ miles

5 hours

1350 feet of ascent

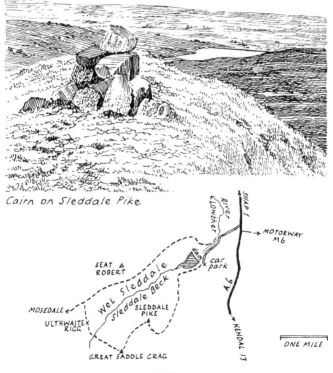

Cairn on Sleddale Pike

Wet Sleddale, although wholly within the National Park, is relatively little known. It bisects Shap Fells, running northeast away from Lakeland to the limestone uplands beyond. The main road A.6, the motorway M6 and the railway all pass near the entrance to the valley, but it is a dead-end for traffic and its mile-long ribbon of tarmac has no signposted attraction to divert speeding motorists. Indeed, its visual appeal has been diminished in the past decade by the construction of a massive dam, for the valley has been taken over by Manchester to augment the water supply to Haweswater. The dam is large but the reservoir is small, and beyond the drowned area with its sad relics and ruins the head of the valley remains unchanged, copses and woodlands relieving the drab backcloth of grassy fells. In the valley bottom the ancient deer enclosures, unique in the district, are safe from engulfment; a new feature nearby is an attractive packhorse bridge built to replace an old one lower down the beck and within the maw of the reservoir. The hills are unaffected, and as they always have been: wild, desolate, even lonelier with the closure of farms.

The deer enclosures

The walk described is long, but easy except for a mile of thick heather and of gentle gradients. It is best done clockwise, as directed, to obtain the advantage of the simple return afforded by an old high-level bridleway. There is a tarmac road to the dam, where a rough carpark marks the end of wheeled progress. This is the place to pull your boots on.

The Lunch House

Gray Bull

Persons over 75 years of age
are advised to regard it
as unclimbable

TARN CRAG   KENTMERE   HARTER FELL   BRANSTREE
             PIKE

Mosedale
Quarry

view west from Sleddale Pike

244

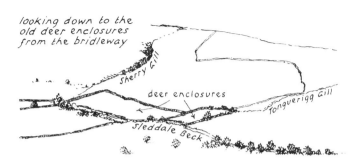

looking down to the
old deer enclosures
from the bridleway

Sherry Gill

deer enclosures

Tonguerigg Gill

Sleddale Beck

the new reservoir in Wet Sleddale, from the bridleway

new 'packhorse' bridge, Sleddale Beck
(erected by Manchester Corporation)

245

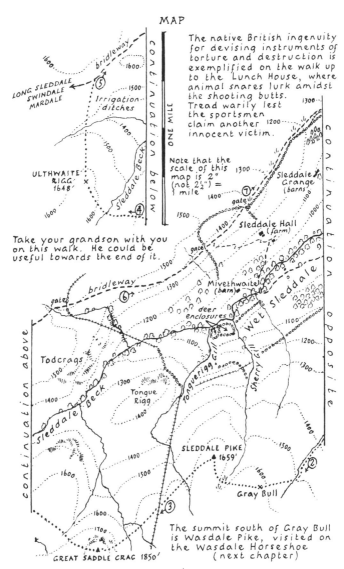

MAP

The native British ingenuity for devising instruments of torture and destruction is exemplified on the walk up to the Lunch House, where animal snares lurk amidst the shooting butts. Tread warily lest the sportsmen claim another innocent victim.

Note that the scale of this map is 2" (not 2½") = 1 mile

LONG SLEDDALE SWINDALE MARDALE

bridleway

1600

1600

1500

Irrigation ditches

1400

1500

ULTHWAITE RIGG 1648' x

1600

Sleddale Beck

1600

continuation below

ONE MILE

1300

1200

1100

1300

Sleddale Grange (barns

1400

gate

Sleddale Hall (farm)

continuation opposite

1500

gate

1400

1300

Take your grandson with you on this walk. He could be useful towards the end of it.

bridleway

gate

1300

Mivethwaite (barn)

Wet Sleddale

deer enclosures

1100

1200

1200

Todcrags

1500

1400

Sleddale Beck

1300

Tongue Rigg

Tonguerigg Gill

Sherry Gill

1300

1300

1400

1400

1400

SLEDDALE PIKE ▲ 1659'

1500

1600

1500

1300

1600

1400

Gray Bull x

1600

1700

The summit south of Gray Bull is Wasdale Pike, visited on the Wasdale Horseshoe (next chapter)

GREAT SADDLE CRAG 1850'

246

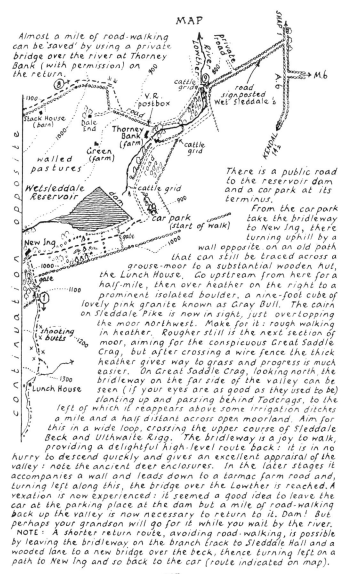

MAP

Almost a mile of road-walking can be 'saved' by using a private bridge over the river at Thorney Bank (with permission) on the return.

SHAP ↑

private road

River Lowther

→ M.6

cattle grid

road signposted Wet Sleddale 2

A.6

KENDAL 14½

900

800

⑧

V.R. postbox

road

Thorney Bank (farm)

1000

Stack House (barn)

Dale End

Green (farm)

walled pastures

cattle grid

900

1000

1300

Wetsleddale Reservoir

dam

cattle grid

car park (start of walk)

gate

1000

New Ing

gate

1100

shooting butts

1200

1300

Lunch House

continuation opposite

There is a public road to the reservoir dam and a car park at its terminus.

From the car park take the bridleway to New Ing, there turning uphill by a wall opposite on an old path that can still be traced across a grouse-moor to a substantial wooden hut, the Lunch House. Go upstream from here for a half-mile, then over heather on the right to a prominent isolated boulder, a nine-foot cube of lovely pink granite known as Gray Bull. The cairn on Sleddale Pike is now in sight, just overtopping the moor northwest. Make for it: rough walking in heather. Rougher still is the next section of moor, aiming for the conspicuous Great Saddle Crag, but after crossing a wire fence the thick heather gives way to grass and progress is much easier. On Great Saddle Crag, looking north, the bridleway on the far side of the valley can be seen (if your eyes are as good as they used to be) slanting up and passing behind Todcrags, to the left of which it reappears above some irrigation ditches a mile and a half distant across open moorland. Aim for this in a wide loop, crossing the upper course of Sleddale Beck and Ulthwaite Rigg. The bridleway is a joy to walk, providing a delightful high-level route back: it is in no hurry to descend quickly and gives an excellent appraisal of the valley: note the ancient deer enclosures. In the later stages it accompanies a wall and leads down to a tarmac farm road and, turning left along this, the bridge over the Lowther is reached. A vexation is now experienced: it seemed a good idea to leave the car at the parking place at the dam but a mile of road-walking back up the valley is now necessary to return to it. Dam! But perhaps your grandson will go for it while you wait by the river.

NOTE: A shorter return route, avoiding road-walking, is possible by leaving the bridleway on the branch track to Sleddale Hall and a wooded lane to a new bridge over the beck, thence turning left on a path to New Ing and so back to the car (route indicated on map).

247

The Wasdale Horseshoe

visiting
  Whatshaw Common, 1593'
  Little Yarlside, 1691'
  Great Yarlside, 1986'
  Wasdale Pike, 1852'

1150 feet of ascent

from the A6
ROAD SUMMIT

5¾ miles
3 hours

Great Yarlside, from Little Yarlside

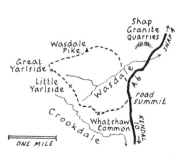

ONE MILE

Great Yarlside
and Little Yarlside
from Whatshaw Common

Wasdale and Wasdale Head are magical names to all Lakeland fellwalkers— not many of whom, however, know that they are repeated within the National Park on the eastern fringe of the region. The names are the same, the scenery different. In the Wasdale of Shap Fells are no high mountains but only rolling hills of gentle gradient, no cliffs of naked rock except for a granite quarry, not a scree-run in sight, no challenging tracks and no excitement. Here is featureless desolation, and solitude, and silence; and were it not for that once-busy ribbon of tarmac, the A.6, this would seem a no-man's-land, a wilderness relieved by a few stone walls. Even the A.6 has lost its voice. .... Easy walking country, but lonely.

The head of this Wasdale is a skyline formed by four fell-tops, of which Great Yarlside is not only the loftiest but the most significant, being on a main watershed between the catchment areas of the Eden and the Lune.   The walk described links these four summits, and because it starts from the highest part of the A.6, at 1400', the amount of climbing is small.   Old men tend to prefer elevated starting places that can be reached on wheels; this is one of the handiest.

The summit of
Wasdale Pike

249

Almost all the trigonometrical survey stations are indicated by columns of concrete or rough stone and it is unusual to find one marked only by a circular metal plate sunk into concrete at ground level.

Such a one occurs on Great Yarlside, a few paces from the highest point and on the west side of the wall crossing the summit.

The Ordnance Survey has recently had a change of mind about the altitude of Great Yarlside. For years the height was recorded as 1937' although the highest contour on their 2½" map was 1975'. In current issues of their 1" map the height is given as 1986', an overdue recognition that must have pleased Great Yarlside and its few admirers.

The summit contours on the 2½" map appear to be too closely drawn and exaggerate the steepness.

Those who walk the Wasdale Horseshoe expecting a panoramic view of Lakeland will be disappointed.

Great Yarlside is the best viewpoint reached on the route, but even here the fells around the head of Long Sleddale and Mardale, not seen at their best, conceal what lies beyond and only to the south of Grey Crag is there a distant vista — to the Coniston range.

Eastwards, however, the prospect is far ranging, from Cross Fell southwards along the spine of the Pennines.

This perched boulder, resting on a massive plinth of pink granite, rejoices in the name (according to the Ordnance Survey) of TO STONE OR TO'THER, which doesn't make sense in the local dialect. One wonders whether the surveyor heard his informant aright — 'ONE STONE ON T'OTHER' or 'TOP STONE ON T'OTHER' would be appropriate and understandable.

The map on page 6 shows its location: it is offroute and not worth a detour because of its boggy defences.

Ruins of
Wasdale Head
farmhouse

This walk is easy but pathless, and lies over unfrequented terrain. Accompanying fences make it safe in mist, but in such conditions there is no pleasure in doing it. Take a pal.

Leave the A.6 on Shap Summit near its solitary building, a substation 100 yards north of an ample layby, crossing both a wire road fence (with difficulty, if short-legged) and a wood snow-fence to tackle the easy gradient of Whatshaw Common, inclining left to join the wall running up and over the fell: a grass road, once a highway but now barely recognisable, is crossed on this climb. The stone wall alternates with a wire fence along the top. A boghole with a protective fence (for the safety of sheep, not humans) is the only feature. After passing the main summit (highest point on the south side of the wall, but not worth a visit) the stone wall persists down into the depression of Wasdale Mouth, patterned by irrigation ditches, and having a fine view up Crookdale.

GREY CRAG

WASDALE PIKE 1852'

continuation on opposite page

peat hags

1800

1700

1600

1500

1400

1300

③

GREAT YARLSIDE 1986' ×

Yarlside Crag

1900

1800

②

1700

1600

1500

Little Yarlside × 1691'

1300

Wasdale Mouth

The wall goes forward, with you alongside, over the grassy top of Little Yarlside and then on rougher ground, to Great Yarlside. There is no cairn on the highest point (on the west side of the wall) but nearby, and 10 yards from the wall, a metal plate of the Ordnance Survey is sunk into the turf. Go on to the wall end and follow the wire fence running east, crossing this at any convenient place to visit the top of Wasdale Pike, which has two cairns and a raingauge 40 yards south of the main one. But in mist keep to the fence.

Crookdale Beck

Crookdale

1400

1500

1300

Descend from Wasdale Pike by a thin track along a strip of grass amidst heather until it ceases on rougher ground above Wasdale Head Farm: take direction from the tall mast ahead until the farm is sighted. Go down to the farm, a sad ruin, and follow an abandoned access road to a gate on the A.6. Turn right for half a mile to the starting point.

R To stone or to'ther (see note on page 4)

MAP

1400

x mast

stake

④

1700

1800

Shap Granite Quarries

1600

1700

1500

A.6

Wasdale Head (derelict farm)

gates

1400

gate

1300

⑤

A.6 1200 SHAP 5

Wasdale

gate

Wasdale Beck

1200

new plantation

Surprisingly, the road summit is not the main watershed. This is proved by the course of Wasdale Beck, which runs north of it but is a feeder of the south-flowing River Lune.

1200

1300

1400

1500

old road

G.P.O. telephone substation

layby

road summit 1397'

①

bog

The road summit is provided with extensive parking places: relics of pre-motorway days, when it was a popular halt for heavy transport.

x 1589'

x 1593' Whatshaw Common

A.6 KENDAL 10

A bus service (Kendal-Penrith) operates along the A.6.

ONE MILE

continuation on opposite page

The Crookdale Horseshoe

visiting

Lord's Seat, 1719'
Robin Hood, 1613'
High House Bank, 1627'

1300 feet of ascent

from HUCK'S BRIDGE

8 miles
4½ hours

High House Bank

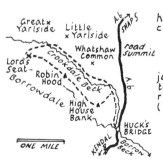

Normally one thinks of a horseshoe walk as a high-level circuit of the ridges enclosing a valley.   This Crookdale tour does not quite measure up to the qualifications: it is low-level on the outward journey, following the valley up to reach one of the enclosing ridges for the return journey. (The ridge omitted is used on the previous chapter's walk).

This is a walk to be done in dry weather only.   Rain in Crookdale does nothing for the morale.

Crookdale Beck pursues a sinuous course of loops and bends from its headwaters on Grey Crag to its emergence from the shallow valley it has carved, and nowhere in the five-mile journey occur any features worthy of mention to relieve the drab monotony of the enclosing slopes, too gently graded to be exciting, and the marshy valley floor, of which in a lifetime one experience is enough. All is grass, and most of it is wet grass. Yet Crookdale has a certain beauty, the beauty of desolation, when the westering sun burnishes its miles of prairie. A few sheep are the only signs of life; there is sluggish movement in the beck. This is a valley without a habitation and the loneliest within the National Park.

On the north side is the Yarlside ridge, rising from the road-summit of the A.6 and continuing to the mass of Grey Crag at the head of the valley. The south side is a parallel ridge of three summits with gentle gradients, providing simple walking and a survey of the valleys on either side, but in other directions the views are disappointing, of Lakeland especially, Grey Crag and Ill Bell being seen but little else.

Crookdale and
Great Yarlside

Hause Foot

Note the rounded boulders of pink granite scattered in the vicinity of Hause Foot: two miles north are the well-known Shap Granite Quarries. The old road over Shap Fells crossed the bridge at Hause Foot on the final climb to the hause (pass), hence the name.

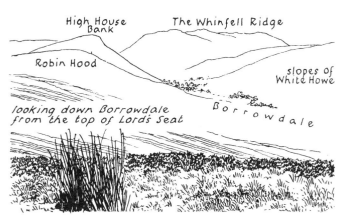

High House Bank   The Whinfell Ridge

Robin Hood   slopes of White Howe

looking down Borrowdale
from the top of Lord's Seat   B o r r o w d a l e

The beacon on Robin Hood,
looking to High House Bank

The cairn on High House Bank,
looking down Borrowdale.

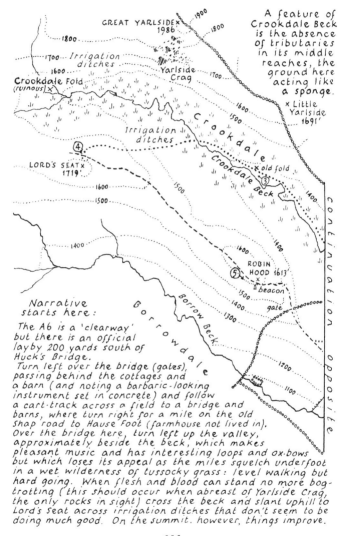

MAP

A feature of
Crookdale Beck
is the absence
of tributaries
in its middle
reaches, the
ground here
acting like
a sponge.

GREAT YARLSIDE×
1986

1900

1800

1800

1700 *Irrigation*

1600 *ditches*

Yarlside
Crag

1700

Crookdale Fold
(ruinous)×

1600

1500

Crookdale

× Little
Yarlside
1691'

Irrigation
ditches

④

LORD'S SEAT×
1719'

Crookdale Beck

× old fold

③

1600

1500

1400

1500

1400

1600

1600

ROBIN
HOOD 1613
⑤
△ beacon

1500

1400

gate

1300

continuation opposite

Borrow Beck

Borrowdale

1200

1100

Narrative
starts here:

 The A6 is a 'clearway'
but there is an official
layby 200 yards south of
Huck's Bridge.
 Turn left over the bridge (gates),
passing behind the cottages and
a barn (and noting a barbaric-looking
instrument set in concrete) and follow
a cart-track across a field to a bridge and
barns, where turn right for a mile on the old
Shap road to Hause Foot (farmhouse not lived in).
Over the bridge here, turn left up the valley,
approximately beside the beck, which makes
pleasant music and has interesting loops and ox-bows
but which loses its appeal as the miles squelch underfoot
in a wet wilderness of tussocky grass: level walking but
hard going. When flesh and blood can stand no more bog-
trotting (this should occur when abreast of Yarlside Crag,
the only rocks in sight) cross the beck and slant uphill to
Lord's Seat across irrigation ditches that don't seem to be
doing much good. On the summit, however, things improve.

258

Narrative continued:

Lord's Seat, the turning point of the walk, is a nice dry perch (no cairn) with a fine view down Borrowdale, and it is blessed with a cart-track that crosses the summit and gives excellent walking along the ridge to Robin Hood and beyond a gate in a crosswall, but when it turns off to descend into Borrowdale (this being the quickest way back to the car) keep on the ridge, crossing a fence at a gate and climbing up to the top of High House Bank (the 1400' contour on O.S. maps is wrong here).

MAP

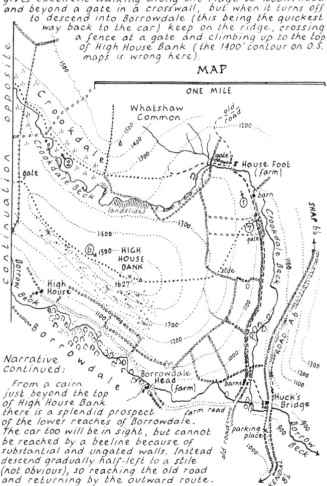

ONE MILE

Crookdale

Whatshaw Common

old road

1200

1500

1400

1300

gate

House Foot (farm)

barn

landslides

Crookdale Beck

1300

SHAP 6½

1400

(6) 1500   HIGH HOUSE BANK

gate

stile

1100

ROAD A6

High House

1627

Borrow Beck

1100

1300

1200

1000

KENDAL 8½

1300

1200

1100

Narrative continued:

From a cairn just beyond the top of High House Bank there is a splendid prospect of the lower reaches of Borrowdale. The car too will be in sight, but cannot be reached by a beeline because of substantial and ungated walls. Instead descend gradually half-left to a stile (not obvious), so reaching the old road and returning by the outward route.

Borrowdale Head (farm)

barns

farm road

Huck's Bridge

old road

parking place

900

900

Borrow Beck

1000

continuation opposite

Continuation continued:

259

The Bannisdale Horseshoe

visiting

Whiteside Pike, 1302'
Todd Fell, 1313'
Capplebarrow, 1683'
a nameless summit, 1819'
a nameless summit, 1771'
Long Crag, 1602'
White Howe, 1737'
a nameless summit, 1736'
Lamb Pasture, 1205'

2,000 feet of ascent

from the
BANNISDALE ROAD

11½ miles

7 hours

Bannisdale Head

1771' x
Long Crag x
1819 x
White Howe x
x 1736'
Borrowdale
Bannisdale Beck
Bannisdale
Capplebarrow
Long Sleddale
Todd Fell x
Lamb Pasture
SHAP 8
A 6
Whiteside Pike x
MOSER
PLOUGH INN
KENDAL 5
ONE MILE

The cairn on Whiteside Pike

Bannisdale

Several valleys cut deeply through the upland wilderness of Shap Fells, fanning out like the spokes of a wheel from a common plateau at the head of Long Sleddale. These valleys are seldom visited but are impressively seen in succession on a journey along the A6 road — with one exception: Bannisdale, which hides behind a screen of trees and is unnoticed by passing travellers although in fact forming a profound and clearly defined cutting through the hills over a four-mile length. Another factor contributing to Bannisdale's seclusion is the stratagem adopted by its solitary road, which does not enter the valley directly but, without a clue as to its destination, slants across the fellside into the hidden recesses of the valley from a distant point on the A6. Such subterfuges do not deceive Manchester's engineers, who have an instinct for locating shy valleys; in recent years trial holes for a dam have been sunk and, although the threat is not imminent, rain-gauges are maintained here. Meanwhile, Bannisdale earns a living for two farms deeply set in the shelter of a surround of fells. The lofty skyline forms a horseshoe, consistently above 1500' for five miles, and provides a good high-level walk all around the valley, being bounded on the outside, west by Long Sleddale and east by Borrowdale, so that the traverse overlooks three parallel valleys. The watershed is everywhere grassy — a sheep pasture enjoyed also by fell ponies — and featureless, one mile being very much like the next except for the distinctive Whiteside Pike, a dark pyramid of heather and bracken and outcrops of rock: much the most attractive part of the horseshoe and worth a visit even if one goes no further.

The approach to Whiteside Pike

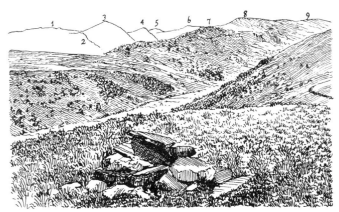

Long Sleddale, from Todd Fell

1 : Yoke
2 : Rainsborrow Crag
3 : Ill Bell
4 : Froswick
5 : Caudale Moor
6 : Thornthwaite Crag
7 : Shipman Knotts
8 : Kentmere Pike
9 : Harter Fell

Long Sleddale, from Capplebarrow

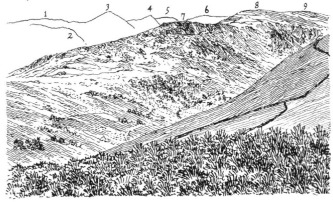

Dryhowe Bridge

Bannisdale Beck, near Lowbridge House

Bannisdale, from Lamb Pasture

The Walk

NOTE VERY WELL INDEED that this is a walk *only for the superbly fit*. Being pure in heart is not enough. It is the longest walk in this book and a gruelling test for old age pensioners, a marathon the safe accomplishment of which is a merited occasion for ribald rejoicing; while those who perish on the way must be content with the lesser gratification of knowing they died with their boots on.

It is a circuit of the valley of Bannisdale, and follows the watershed around it. The gradients are simple, with no steep sections, and no difficulty in route-finding occurs. The scenery is desolate and has little of beauty. The only exciting situations arise in the climbing of two walls and an awkward new fence on White Howe, mentioned on page 267* — there are no other hazards except those that result from wet feet. It is a slog over grassy prairies: a splendid exercise for the legs and tonic for the ego, but not enriching to the eyes or the mind. You do it because it is there, as somebody once said, and to prove to yourself and to the sceptic next door that there is life in the old dog yet.

Plan it like planning a military campaign, to a timetable and with due regard to resources. Take a companion who is agile enough to run for help,.... Allow a full day to provide time for halts for iron ration snacks and frequent prayers for survival.

God be with you.

* Come to think of it, the Kendal Ramblers, who are always ready to do a good deed, may volunteer to erect, with the farmer's permission, a simple step-stile over this fence. It's just a thought. After all, they'll be old themselves someday.

Same scale on the
next three pages

ONE MILE

continuation on page 266   continuation on page 267

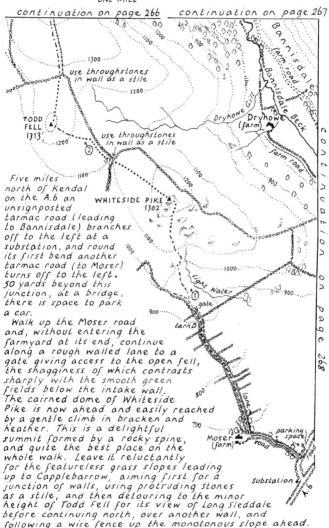

1300

use throughstones
in wall as a stile

1200

1100

TODD
FELL
1313

1200

use throughstones
in wall as a stile

②

1100

900

Bannisdale

farm road

Bannisdale Beck

Dryhowe Gill

Dryhowe
(farm)

farm road

WHITESIDE PIKE ▲
1302

1100

1200

1100

1000

1000

Light Water

①

gate

900

tarn

900

lane

800

700

Moser
(farm)

road

parking
space

x

substation

A.6

continuation on page 268

Five miles
north of Kendal
on the A.6 an
unsignposted
tarmac road (leading
to Bannisdale) branches
off to the left at a
substation, and round
its first bend another
tarmac road (to Moser)
turns off to the left.
50 yards beyond this
junction, at a bridge,
there is space to park
a car.

 Walk up the Moser road
and, without entering the
farmyard at its end, continue
along a rough walled lane to a
gate giving access to the open fell,
the shagginess of which contrasts
sharply with the smooth green
fields below the intake wall.
The cairned dome of Whiteside
Pike is now ahead and easily reached
by a gentle climb in bracken and
heather. This is a delightful
summit formed by a rocky spine,
and quite the best place on the
whole walk. Leave it reluctantly
for the featureless grass slopes leading
up to Capplebarrow, aiming first for a
junction of walls, using protruding stones
as a stile, and then detouring to the minor
height of Todd Fell for its view of Long Sleddale
before continuing north, over another wall, and
following a wire fence up the monotonous slope ahead.

265

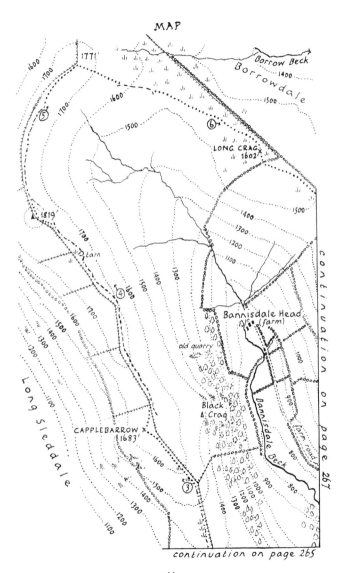

MAP

Borrow Beck

Borrowdale

1400

1500

1771'

1600

1700

1700

1600

⑤

1500

⑥

LONG CRAG
1602'

1500

1400

1300

1200

1100

1500

▲1819'

1700

Tarn

1600

④

1500

1400

1700

1600

Bannisdale Head
(farm)

1500

1400

1300

1200

1000

old quarry

Black
△ Crag

900

Bannisdale Beck

farm road

Long Sleddale

CAPPLEBARROW x
1683'

1600

1500

1400

1300

1200

1100

③

1400

1300

1200

1100

1000

900

800

continuation on page 267

continuation on page 265

In due course the tedium of the long grassy climb (the only feature met being an abandoned roll of fence wire) is relieved by arrival on the summit of Capplebarrow and a sudden view of the head of Long Sleddale beyond; there is no cairn. Now (unless feeling weary, in which case a retracing of steps to the car is advised) cross the fence to take advantage of a tractor track on the other side and resume the journey north. A hidden tarn makes a welcome change of scene and is a good place to halt; skirt it on the east side and continue, uphill again, by the side of the fence (here large-mesh wire, a source of danger to horned sheep: disentangle any found trapped by it). The top of this rise is the highest point of the walk (1819') but not even yet is it time to turn southwards. Still head north by the fence (now joined by a broken wall) across a shallow depression to the top of the next rise, at 1771'. This is the turning point at last: the farthest limit of Bannisdale; ahead is

the Borrowdale catchment area backed by Grey Crag with the rockface of Mere Crag prominent on its lower slopes. Aim now for Long Crag, getting a view down Bannisdale en route and looking for the fell ponies that graze over its upper reaches. Long Crag is rather a mess, being defended by a moat of peat-hags and marshes. Pass through gaps in two crosswalls beyond and then climb an easy slope to the Ordnance column on White Howe, a splendid viewpoint. A twin height continues the ridge to the south and a wide break in an intervening wall indicates the route thereto but is found to be guarded by a new wire-mesh fence topped with barbed wire: the farmer, knowing that few hikers ever come this way and obviously unaware that it might, from 1974 onwards, become a popular walk for old men, has not provided a stile (which seems a little ungrateful if you have just rescued his sheep). The fence is too high to cock a leg over and can be negotiated only at some peril, although a desperate man who has lost all respect for his private parts will be over it in a jiffy. A tractor track leads up to point 1736' from the gap and descends the far side; when it fades bear east of south to avoid crags ahead.

On the map:
MAP
1500
gap
1600
1700
WHITE HOWE 1737'
1600
1500
gap in wall but not in fence
1600
1736' x
1700
1200
1100
1000
1500
1600
Bannisdale
farm road
800
900

continuation on page 266

continuation on page 265   and 268

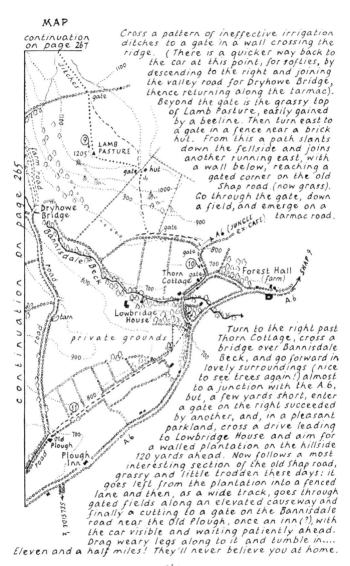

continuation on page 267

Cross a pattern of ineffective irrigation ditches to a gate in a wall crossing the ridge. (There is a quicker way back to the car at this point, for softies, by descending to the right and joining the valley road for Dryhowe Bridge, thence returning along the tarmac.) Beyond the gate is the grassy top of Lamb Pasture, easily gained by a beeline. Then turn east to a gate in a fence near a brick hut. From this a path slants down the fellside and joins another running east, with a wall below, reaching a gated corner on the old Shap road (now grass). Go through the gate, down a field, and emerge on a tarmac road.

continuation on page 265

1100

ditches

gate

1100

⑨ LAMB PASTURE
1205

gate hut

1000

900

Dryhowe Bridge

900

gate

A.6 (JUNGLE ex-CAFÉ)

gate 800

Thorn gate ⑩ 700
Cottage SHAP 9

700 Forest Hall (farm)

800 700 A.6

tarn

Lowbridge House

private grounds

900 700

⑪

800

Old Plough
Plough Inn A.6

road

SEDBERGH 2

Bannisdale Beck

road

Turn to the right past Thorn Cottage, cross a bridge over Bannisdale Beck, and go forward in lovely surroundings (nice to see trees again!) almost to a junction with the A.6, but, a few yards short, enter a gate on the right succeeded by another, and, in a pleasant parkland, cross a drive leading to Lowbridge House and aim for a walled plantation on the hillside 120 yards ahead. Now follows a most interesting section of the old Shap road, grassy and little trodden these days: it goes left from the plantation into a fenced lane and then, as a wide track, goes through gated fields along an elevated causeway and finally a cutting to a gate on the Bannisdale road near the Old Plough, once an inn(?), with the car visible and waiting patiently ahead. Drag weary legs along to it and tumble in....

Eleven and a half miles! They'll never believe you at home.

THE VIEW

The view of Lakeland is almost the same from all the main summits of the horseshoe. On the whole it is rather disappointing, much being concealed by the Kentmere and Long Sleddale hills.

Principal Lakeland Fells	from WHITESIDE PIKE	from CAPPLEBARROW	from WHITE HOWE
Whiteside Pike	-	✓	✓
Black Combe	✓	✓	✓
The Coniston range	✓	✓	✓
Crinkle Crags	✓	✓	✓
Scafell	✓	✓	✓
Bowfell	✓	✓	✓
Scafell Pike			✓
Great End	✓	✓	✓
Great Gable	✓	✓	✓
Langdale Pikes	✓	✓	✓
High Raise	✓	✓	
Yoke	✓		✓
Red Screes			
Ill Bell	✓	✓	
Froswick	✓	✓	
Caudale Moor	✓	✓	
Thornthwaite Crag	✓	✓	
Kentmere Pike	✓	✓	✓
Harter Fell	✓	✓	✓
Capplebarrow	✓	-	✓
Tarn Crag	✓	✓	✓
Grey Crag	✓	✓	✓
White Howe	✓	✓	-
Skeggles Water	✓	✓	

In other directions, mainly east and south, the panorama is very extensive, including a continuous skyline of the Pennines ranging from Cross Fell south to Pendle Hill with the Howgills prominent.

The town of Kendal is visible in its green valley; beyond is the Kent Estuary issuing into Morecambe Bay.

Ordnance column S5671 White Howe

The White Howe ridge from Dryhowe Bridge

INDEX OF NAMED FELLS AND SUMMITS

The page reference is the first page of the relevant chapter

KNOTT, THE	...	...	150
LAMB PASTURE	...	...	260
LANGHOWE PIKE	...	...	236
LATTERBARROW	...	...	84
LITTLE YARLSIDE	...	...	248
LONG CRAG	...	...	260
LORD'S SEAT	...	...	36
LORD'S SEAT	...	...	254
LOW LIGHT HAW	...	...	92
MUNCASTER FELL	...	...	186
NABS MOOR	...	...	230
NEWTON FELL	...	...	52
ORREST HEAD	...	...	26
PIKE, THE	...	...	140
PIKES	...	...	120
PONSONBY FELL	...	...	192
POTTER FELL	...	...	8
RAVEN'S BARROW	...	...	42
RESTON SCAR	...	...	24
ROBIN HOOD	...	...	254
ROUGH CRAG	...	...	144
ST. JOHN'S HILL	...	...	206
SCALEBARROW KNOTT	...	...	224
SCHOOL KNOTT	...	...	30
SCOUT SCAR	...	...	2
SEAT HOW	...	...	144
SEAT ROBERT	...	...	236
SETMURTHY COMMON	...	...	202
SLEDDALE PIKE	...	...	242
STAINTON PIKE	...	...	150
STAVELEY FELL	...	...	48
STICKLE PIKE	...	...	126
STOUPDALE HEAD	...	...	162
TARN HILL	...	...	126
TODD FELL	...	...	260
TOP O' SELSIDE	...	...	92
TOTTLEBANK HEIGHT.	...	...	108
ULGRAVES	...	...	8
ULTHWAITE RIGG	...	...	242
WALNA SCAR	...	...	114
WASDALE PIKE	...	...	248
WATCH HILL	...	...	202
WATER CRAG	...	...	144
WHATSHAW COMMON	...	...	248
WHITBARROW	...	...	36
WHITE COMBE	...	...	162
WHITE HOWE	...	...	260
WHITE PIKE	...	...	144
WHITESIDE PIKE	...	...	260
WHIT FELL	...	...	156
WILLIAMSON'S MONUMENT.			18
WOODEND HEIGHT	...	...	144
WOODLAND FELL	...	...	102
WOOL KNOTT	...	...	102
YEW BANK	...	...	102
YOADCASTLE	...	...	144

READER'S PERSONAL LOG

This and the next five pages are designed
for the use of readers who wish to keep a
personal record of their performance
of the walks detailed in the book

Walk	Date	Time		Participants ~~Companions~~ →	Weather
		start	finish		
Scout Scar					
Potter Fell					
Green Quarter Fell					
High Knott					
Hugill Fell					
Reston Scar					

Walk	Date	Time		Companions	Weather
		start	finish		
Orrest Head	7/13/10	11:00	12:30	Mom & Nat	Cool & Cloudy
School Knott					
Brant Fell					
Whitbarrow					
Cartmel Fell					
Gummer's How					
Staveley Fell					
Newton Fell					
Hampsfell	7/15/10	10:00	12:00	Mom & Nat	Cool & Wet
Humphrey Head					

Walk	Date	Time		Companions	Weather
		start	finish		
Bigland Barrow					
Finsthwaite Heights					
Claife Heights					
Latterbarrow					
Carron Crag					
Top o' Selside					
Beacon Fell					
Woodland Fell					
Blawith Knott					
Burney					

Walk	Date	Time		Companions	Weather
		start	finish		
Walna Scar					
Caw					
Stickle Pike					
Dunnerdale Fells					
Great Worm Crag					
Hesk Fell					
The Circuit of Devoke Water					
Stainton Pike					
Whit Fell					
Black Combe					

Walk	Date	Time		Companions	Weather
		start	finish		
Boat How					
Irton Pike					
Muncaster Fell					
Ponsonby Fell					
Cold Fell					
Flat Fell and Dent					
Watch Hill					
Clints Crags					
Caermote Hill					
Faulds Brow					

Walk	Date	Time		Companions	Weather
		start	finish		
Dunmallet					
Heughscar Hill					
Knipescar Common					
The Naddle Horseshoe					
Howes					
Seat Robert					
The Wet Sleddale Horseshoe					
The Wasdale Horseshoe					
The Crookdale Horseshoe					
The Bannisdale Horseshoe					

SYMBOLS

ON THE ROUTE MAPS

Route on motor road   *Unenclosed* ~~~~~
                                  Enclosed ~~~~~

Good footpath
(sufficiently distinct to be followed in mist)

Intermittent footpath
(difficult to follow in mist)

No path : route recommended

Wall   oooooooooooo   Broken wall   o o o o o o o o o o o

Fence   ++++++++++   Broken fence   ı ı ı ı ı ı ı ı ı ı ı

Marshy ground   ⊥ ⊥ ⊥ ⊥ ⊥ ⊥ ⊥   Trees

Crags   ⋂⋂ ⋂⋂   Scree   Boulders

Stream or River
(arrow indicates direction of flow)

Waterfall   Bridge

Buildings   ▪▬ ▪▪   Unenclosed road

Summit cairn   ▲   Other (prominent) cairns   △   △

Ordnance column   △   Limestone clints

Contours (at 100' intervals)   ⋯ 900 ⋯   Railway

Miles from starting point   ④

O.S : Ordnance Survey
Y.H : Youth Hostel

On all maps, north is top of the page.

Heights of fells, *where stated in the book but not confirmed by the Ordnance maps, are approximate*

278